Developing Science Writing Skills

BY
MYRL SHIREMAN

COPYRIGHT © 2009 Mark Twain Media, Inc.

ISBN 978-1-58037-485-9

Printing No. CD-404104

Mark Twain Media, Inc., Publishers
Distributed by Carson-Dellosa Publishing Company, Inc.

Visit us at www.carsondellosa.com

The purchase of this book entitles the buyer to reproduce the student pages for classroom use only. Other permissions may be obtained by writing Mark Twain Media, Inc., Publishers.

All rights reserved. Printed in the United States of America.

Table of Contents

Introduction

The National Science Standards speak to the necessity for students to develop skills in producing oral and written reports. The National Council of Teachers Standards for English and Language Arts stress that it is important for students to develop writing and speaking skills to communicate effectively with a variety of audiences and for different purposes. Effective oral and written reports in science must accurately present the scientific data in a concise manner. In oral and written science reports, students must have key basic writing skills. Used properly, these key writing skills make science reports more powerful.

The most important objective when presenting oral and written science reports is to inform. Science reports are not presented to persuade. The main objective of the report is not to entertain. Oral and written science reports must convey specific information in an objective manner. The listeners and readers are not always scientists, so the reports must be presented with clarity.

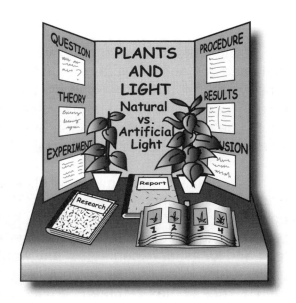

Students in Grades 5–8 are developing skills in stating a hypothesis and explanations to be presented in their science classes. The students are orally explaining the experiment to be performed. They are writing summaries explaining their experiment results. Students present oral and written summaries of data from graphs and charts. The reports are much more powerful when presented using the appropriate oral and written skills.

Science activities in *Developing Science Writing Skills* are developed around the National Science Standards for Grades 5–8, including the use of metrics. The writing activities in *Developing Science Writing Skills* are designed to develop the foundation oral and written skills recommended for oral and written science reports. The key foundation skills are stressed because many students in Grades 5–8 do not yet have these skills. They will need the skills if they are to become effective speakers and writers in later grades. Teachers can implement differentiated instruction strategies by varying the amount of teacher-led instruction given. For students who need more guidance, teachers can model the skills and lead students through the activities by making the worksheets into transparencies. Students who can work more independently can complete the activities in small groups or on their own. Activities require minimum teacher time in grading written work. The activities are designed so that students assume a role of correcting reports by other students.

Introduction (cont.)

For most students, science writing skills do not come naturally. The skills must be developed step-by-step. Students must have ample opportunity to recognize and practice particular skills prior to a full writing assignment. In science reports, summaries, and explanations, students must be able to accurately use key basic writing skills.

The activities are designed so students develop skills in accurately using present and past tense, active and passive voice constructions, and writing sentences that make a specific point. Activities to develop an understanding of how coordinating conjunctions can be used to develop sentences with greater clarity are also included.

Students who write effective science reports understand basic sentence structure so that each sentence is written to make a specific point. An understanding of how to use present tense and past tense with specific types of science reports is a necessity. Students must be able to use active and passive voice to make sentences more powerful. Science reporting should be direct and to the point. Students must refrain from slang and figurative language in science writing. They must also avoid complex sentence structures.

In order for students to practice and develop their science writing skills, students may want to keep science writing journals. These journals can be notebooks or binders of loose-leaf paper where students do daily or weekly writing related to their science classes, reading, and projects. Students can include writings about questions they have, hypotheses they want to test, and ideas for experiments they want to conduct. This would also be a good place to write rough drafts of the results and any conclusions the students make after performing the experiments. These notes can then be used to prepare the final science report for the classroom or science fair.

When students progress through the science curriculum, the importance of having well-developed writing skills becomes paramount. Well-developed writing skills lead students to become more critical readers. Student science projects at science fairs are evaluated on written accuracy as well as science content. Every science experiment or researched project is chock-full of important data. Once students have mastered the basic skills in science writing, they will be able to present the information they have learned through reading, researching, and experimenting in a clear and effective way.

Chapter I: Science Writing
Clear and to the Point

Keys to Writing Science

Scientists have questions. They form hypotheses. They perform experiments. Scientists often give oral and written reports about their experiments. People who read the written reports may not be scientists. So scientists' writing must be very clear and easy to understand. When presenting an oral or written report, you are not entertaining. You are informing.

Subjects and Predicates

You must make sure your sentences are written to make one point. You must know the subject(s) and verb(s) in your sentences. The subject and verb should be close together. This makes it easier for your reader to understand the points you are making.

The **subject** of a sentence is the person, place, or thing spoken about in the sentence. The subject is a noun, pronoun, or a phrase containing a noun or pronoun.

The **predicate** of a sentence explains something about the person, place, or thing that is the subject. The predicate includes a verb and helpers that tell about the subject.

Directions: Each of the following sentences has a subject and predicate. The verb is part of the predicate. Underline the subject in each of the sentences below. Draw a slash (/) through the verb in each sentence.

1. A screw is a simple machine.

2. Velocity is a measure of speed in a particular direction.

3. Water pressure exerts an upward pressure on a floating

   object.

4. Weight may be measured in a unit of force called a newton.

5. Density is how closely together the atoms in an object are packed.

6. Volume measures how much space an object takes up.

7. Static electricity is a spark of electricity.

8. An atom has neutrons, electrons, and protons.

9. Protons and neutrons are found in the nucleus of the atom.

10. Protons have a positive charge.

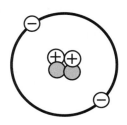

Name: _____ Date: _____

Chapter I: Science Writing
Clear and to the Point (cont.)

Keeping Subjects and Predicates Close Together

In science writing, you want to make the material as easy as possible to understand. Try to write sentences that keep the subject and verb close together. Remember, the verb shows action or state of being. Placing the verb closer to the subject makes it easier for your reader to understand the points you are making.

Directions: Read each of the following sentences. Simplify the sentences by rewriting them to keep the subject and verb close together.

1. An object on the earth's surface weighs more than the same object in space.

   An object _____

2. The force that pulls an object toward the center of the earth is gravity.

   Gravity _____

3. The shape of earth's orbit as the earth travels around the sun is an oval.

   An oval _____

4. The scientific names for what happens to the speed of a thrown ball are acceleration and deceleration.

   Acceleration and deceleration _____

   _____

5. A change in velocity of a thrown ball is known as acceleration.

   Acceleration _____

6. The speed of a falling object is affected by gravity.

   A falling object's _____

7. A rainbow, which appears in the sky when the sun is shining and the atmosphere is full of small droplets of water, is a beautiful sight.

   A rainbow _____

   _____

8. The colored part of the eye is known as the iris.

   The iris _____

Name: _____ Date: _____

Chapter II: Expository Writing

Writing to Inform and Explain

Most of your science writing will be expository. In expository writing, you are writing to answer the questions how or why. You are not trying to persuade. You are writing to inform or explain the important points about a science topic.

Writing Sentences With One Main Point

When writing in science, you want to stick to the main points. You are writing to pass along specific information. You want the reader to understand the material you are writing about. Do not write to entertain. Do not use slang or figurative language. Be very specific. Science writing is more easily understood if you write sentences that contain only a single point.

Directions: Read each of the sentences below. Determine if the sentence makes one point or more than one point. Place a check on the appropriate blank.

1. Volcanoes are found all around the Pacific Ocean coasts.

    ____ one point   ____ more than one point.

2. Static electricity is a result of friction, but it is different from lightning, which jumps from cloud to cloud.   ____ one point   ____ more than one point.

3. Steam forms over a boiling pot as the water vapor cools.

    ____ one point   ____ more than one point.

4. When a ray of white light enters a prism, the ray of white light is bent.

    ____ one point   ____ more than one point.

5. We had a great time completing our experiment on electricity because we all worked together so well.   ____ one point   ____ more than one point.

6. Ice floats because it is less dense than liquid water.

    ____ one point   ____ more than one point.

7. Acceleration is different from speed.

    ____ one point   ____ more than one point.

8. In science, measurements are made using the metric system.

    ____ one point   ____ more than one point.

9. Whooping cranes fly with their huge black-tipped wings flapping gracefully as they migrate from the gulf coast north to Canada each spring.

    ____ one point   ____ more than one point.

10. When oxygen and iron combine, it is a chemical reaction.

    ____ one point   ____ more than one point.

Name: _____ Date: _____

Chapter II: Expository Writing (cont.)

Getting Right to the Main Point

Part 1:

The opening sentence in a paragraph is very important in science writing. Try to make the main point of the paragraph in the opening sentence. Then build with details around the main point.

Directions: From each group of two sentences, select the sentence a) that makes a single point and b) in which the subject and verb are close together. Place a plus (+) on the sentence chosen. Underline the verb in the chosen sentence.

1. ___ a. The earth's crust is a few miles thick.
   ___ b. The earth's crust, only a few miles thick, is made up of large plates.

2. ___ c. The earth's crust, which is thicker under the continents, floats on semi-molten rock below the crust.
   ___ d. The earth's crust is thicker under the continents.

3. ___ e. These large tectonic plates float on semi-molten rock.
   ___ f. Semi-molten rock is below the tectonic plates, and the plates float on it.

4. ___ g. The plates move a few meters and often bump into each other.
   ___ h. The plates move very slowly.

5. ___ i. The earth's crust is made up of 12 large tectonic plates.
   ___ j. Twelve large tectonic plates form the earth's crust, and their edges move against each other.

6. ___ k. Many years ago, the plates separated and formed continents.
   ___ l. The plates separated many years ago.

7. ___ m. The plates move very slowly and cause great change in the earth's surface.
   ___ n. Plate movements cause great changes in the earth's surface.

8. ___ o. When plates bump together, mountains may be formed and earthquakes may cause great destruction.
   ___ p. Large mountain chains are often the result of plates bumping together.

9. ___ q. An example of mountains built by plates bumping together are the Andes Mountains along the west coast of South America, which also affect the climate along the coast.
   ___ r. The Andes Mountains were formed when two plates bumped together.

Name: _____ Date: _____

Chapter II: Expository Writing (cont.)

Getting Right to the Main Point (cont.)

Part 2:

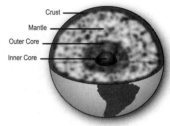

Directions: Select the sentence below that makes the main point of the reading from Part 1 on page 4.

_____ 1. These 12 plates float on semi-molten rock found below the plates.

_____ 2. The plates move.

_____ 3. The earth's crust is make up of 12 large tectonic plates.

_____ 4. When the plates bump together, large mountains may be formed.

_____ 5. The Andes Mountains were formed when two plates bumped together.

Part 3:

Directions: Use the sentences you have selected from Part 1, and write a paragraph for your science writing journal on the lines below. The first sentence should be the main sentence of the paragraph you chose in Part 2. Place the details in order of importance from most important to least important.

_____

_____

_____

_____

_____

_____

_____

_____

_____

_____

_____

Name: _____ Date: _____

Chapter III: Forming the Explanation or Hypothesis

Developing a Hypothesis to Answer the "Why" Question

When a scientist observes something, he or she often wonders why it happens. The scientist has a "why" question. He or she will develop a hypothesis, or explanation, that might explain or answer the "why" question. Then the scientist must develop an experiment to find if the hypothesis is true. The experiment must be limited to one variable that can be tested. The variable can be tested by changing it. During the experiment, the scientist obtains data. Then using the data, he or she develops a conclusion about the hypothesis. After this, the scientist is ready to inform others about the experiment. He or she writes a science report to inform.

Directions: Each of the following questions has been reworded into three possible explanations, or hypotheses. Select the hypothesis that you think is in a form so an experiment could be designed to test the hypothesis.

1. **Question:** Why do the Christmas tree lights still burn when some lights are burned out?
   Hypothesis:
   _____ a. The lightbulbs that stay lighted are a different kind, and they are wired differently.
   _____ b. The lightbulbs that stay lighted are wired on a different circuit than the lightbulbs that burned out.
   _____ c. The lightbulbs that stay lighted have a much stronger filament and are of different brands.

2. **Question:** Why is electromagnet 2 stronger than electromagnets 1 and 3 ?
   Hypothesis:
   _____ a. Electromagnet 3 has a bigger nail, and the nail is made of a different metal.
   _____ b. Electromagnet 1 has a different kind of nail with a different type of wire.
   _____ c. Electromagnet 2 has more loops of wire wrapped around the nail.

3. **Question:** Why does some copper wire resist the flow of electrons more than other copper wire?
   Hypothesis:
   _____ a. Copper wire that is not pure copper and is bent in more than three places resists the flow of electrons more than a straight, pure copper wire.
   _____ b. Copper wire that is kept cold and is wrapped in a coil resists the flow of electrons more than a warm, straight copper wire.
   _____ c. Copper wire with a smaller diameter resists the flow of electrons more than copper wire with a larger diameter.

Name: _____ Date: _____

Chapter III: Forming the
Explanation or Hypothesis (cont.)

4. **Question:** Why does steam form over a pot of boiling water?

   Hypothesis:

   ____ a. Steam forms when water vapor above the pot cools and turns into tiny droplets.

   ____ b. Steam forms when the temperature is 210°F and there are impurities in the air above the pot of boiling water.

   ____ c. Steam forms because the water is hot.

5. **Question:** Why do astronauts float inside the space shuttle?

   Hypothesis:

   ____ a. Astronauts float because they have space suits that are made of very lightweight material, and the astronauts are all small people.

   ____ b. Astronauts float because everything in space floats.

   ____ c. Astronauts float because Earth's gravity is no longer a force on the astronauts in the space shuttle.

6. **Question:** Why do sedimentary rocks, like limestone, have horizontal layers?

   Hypothesis:

   ____ a. Sedimentary rocks have horizontal layers because they are formed by water.

   ____ b. Sedimentary rocks have horizontal layers because each type of sediment settles out of the water at a different rate.

   ____ c. Sedimentary rocks have horizontal layers because they are special rocks.

Name: _____ Date: _____

Chapter IV: Writing the Hypothesis

Writing the Hypothesis

Writing an explanation, or **hypothesis**, is the important first step in developing science experiments. When writing a hypothesis, you must first write down your question. Then rewrite your question as a hypothesis statement. This is a statement that you believe is true and is the answer to the question. Your hypothesis statement should be carefully worded so that you can design an experiment with a variable to test your hypothesis.

Forming a Hypothesis About Prisms and Refracted Light

In Makhi's science class, prisms were being used to refract wavelengths of white light into the rainbow colors. Makhi saw that the rainbow colors from his prism were red, orange, yellow, green, blue, indigo, and violet, in that order. When Makhi observed the colors, he began to think about the prism and the colors.

1. From the three questions below that Makhi developed, select the question you would have asked.

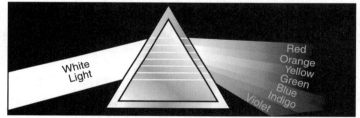

_____ Question A: How does the prism make a ray of white light make the rainbow colors?

_____ Question B: Do the rainbow colors from the prism always appear in the same order?

_____ Question C: Would other prisms make the same colors, or would the colors be different?

2. Write a question of your own about the prism and the rainbow colors.

_____

_____

In science, Makhi knows he must turn his question into a hypothesis that can be tested. Makhi came up with this hypothesis to test Question A. **Hypothesis:** The white light rays are slowed and bent by the prism.

3. Write a hypothesis of your own that could be used to test Question B.

_____

_____

Name: _____ Date: _____

Chapter IV: Writing the Hypothesis (cont.)

Forming a Hypothesis About Electromagnets

Lexus was watching a science program on television. The program was about electromagnets. A large crane was shown moving large pieces of metal from one place to another. A cable with a large flat iron piece was attached to the crane. When the flat iron piece was dropped down, metal was attracted to the large flat iron piece. The crane pulled the large pieces of metal up and swung them to trucks that were waiting. The crane lowered the large pieces of metal down over the trucks. The metal was dropped into the trucks. Lexus began to think about the electromagnet and how it worked.

1. From the two questions below developed by Lexus, select the question you would have asked.

    ____ Question A: If the large flat iron piece was a magnet, why did it lose its magnetic power and drop the metal?

    ____ Question B: How can an electromagnet be made stronger to pick up heavier objects?

2. Write a question of your own about electromagnets.

    _____

    _____

Lexus knows she must turn her question into a hypothesis that can be tested. Lexus came up with this hypothesis to test Question A. **Hypothesis:** An electromagnet is made using an electric current that can be turned on and off.

3. Write a hypothesis of your own that could be used to test Question B.

    _____

    _____

Name: _____ Date: _____

Chapter IV: Writing the Hypothesis (cont.)

Forming Your Own Questions and Hypotheses

Directions: Read each of the following topics, and then write a question you might have about the topic. It could be a question about how something works or how changing one variable affects the process. Then develop a hypothesis that you could use to test your question with an experiment.

1. Sledding

   You are sledding down a long hill. The bottom of the hill is a flat area leading to another hill. Each time your sled reaches the bottom of the hill, the momentum carries you across the flat area and a short distance up the other hill. You ride down the long hill a number of times. However, each time the distance traveled up the next hill is the same.

   Question: _____

   _____

   Hypothesis: _____

   _____

2. A seed sprouting

   Question: _____

   _____

   Hypothesis: _____

   _____

3. Antibacterial soap

   Question: _____

   _____

   Hypothesis: _____

   _____

Name: _____ Date: _____

Chapter V: Designing an Experiment to Test the Hypothesis

Steps in Writing a Science Experiment

Once you have a hypothesis, or explanation, you must design an experiment to test the hypothesis. You must then determine the one variable you will use to test your hypothesis.

Step 1: What is the one variable you will test?

Step 2: How will you change the variable during the experiment?

Step 3: How will you record the data from your experiment?

Step 4: Review the results of your data to determine if your hypothesis is true or false.

Chloe's Die-Tossing Experiment

Chloe is tossing a die. She tosses the die a number of times and observes that the numbers 1 through 6 seem to appear randomly. Chloe began to think about how often a given number would occur when the die was tossed.

Chloe's Question: When a die is tossed, do some numbers appear more often than other numbers?

Chloe's Explanation (Hypothesis): The larger numbers will appear more times than the smaller numbers.

1. Mark whether you agree or disagree with Chloe's hypothesis.

    ____ I agree with Chloe's hypothesis.

    ____ I disagree with Chloe's hypothesis.

2. Write your own hypothesis for the die-tossing experiment.

    _____

    _____

    _____

    _____

    _____

Name: _____   Date: _____

Chapter V: Designing an Experiment to Test the Hypothesis (cont.)

Chloe's Experiment Design for Die Tossing

Chloe decides she will perform an experiment to see how often each of the numbers 1 through 6 appear. Chloe decides she will toss the die 36 times. She decides that she will need the following to complete the experiment: one die and a chart to record the results of the die tosses.

1. Chloe needs help, so she is asking you to toss the die for her and record the number that appears after each toss.

2. On the blanks below, write the number of times each number 1–6 appeared in the table.

    1: _____   2: _____   3: _____   4: _____   5: _____   6: _____

3. Place each number you wrote above as a numerator over the number 36 in the fractions below.

    _____/36   _____/36   _____/36   _____/36   _____/36   _____/36

4. Help Chloe write a summary of her experiment. The summary must tell the results of Chloe's experiment. Write complete sentences in past tense that are to the point and clearly explain the results.

    _____

    _____

    _____

    _____

5. Place a plus (+) on the statement with which you agree.

    ____ Chloe's hypothesis was proven by the experiment.

    ____ Chloe's hypothesis was not proven by the experiment.

6. Explain why you selected that answer. I agree/disagree with Chloe's hypothesis because

    _____

    _____

Name: _____   Date: _____

Chapter V: Designing an Experiment to Test the Hypothesis (cont.)

Wentric's Coin-Flipping Experiment

Wentric flips a coin into the air. The coin lights with a head showing. He flips the coin again and a head is showing. He flips the coin a third time and a head is showing.

Wentric's Question: Will a head appear more times than a tail when a coin is flipped?

Wentric's Hypothesis: There is a difference in the two sides of a coin, so the head will appear more times.

1. Mark whether you agree or disagree with Wentric's hypothesis.

    ____ a. I agree with Wentric's hypothesis.

    ____ b. I disagree with Wentric's hypothesis.

2. Write your hypothesis about the coin flipping. _____

_____

_____

Wentric's Experiment Design

Wentric decided that if he flipped the coin 40 times he could determine if his hypothesis was correct. Wentric decided that he will need a coin and a chart to record the 40 flips, or events. After each flip of the coin, Wentric will write the letter "H" in the chart cell for heads or the letter "T" in the chart cell for tails.

1. Flip the coin for Wentric and record the results.

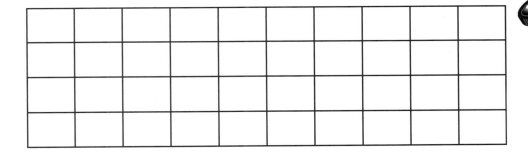

2. Complete the blanks below for the 40 flips of the coin.

    _____/40 heads   _____/40 tails

Name: _____   Date: _____

Chapter V: Designing an Experiment to Test the Hypothesis (cont.)

Wentric's Experiment Design (cont.)

3. Wentric's explanation, or hypothesis, was (correct/incorrect) because _____

    _____

    _____

    _____

4. Help Wentric write a summary of his experiment for his science writing journal. The summary must tell the results of Wentric's experiment. Use complete sentences in past tense that are to the point and clearly explain the results.

    _____

    _____

    _____

    _____

    _____

    _____

    _____

    _____

    _____

    _____

    _____

    _____

    _____

    _____

    _____

    _____

    _____

Name: _____   Date: _____

Chapter VI: Learning to Use Present and Past Tense in Science Writing

Present Tense and Past Tense

When writing in science, it is important to know when to use the present tense and past tense of verbs. The tense of the verb is the time something takes place.

Use **present tense** when something is taking place at the present time.

Examples of present tense:

> The students are in science class.
> > (Students are in class right now.)

> We begin our experiment by heating the water.
> > (The experiment is going on now.)

The **present tense** is also used to talk about things that are constant.

Examples of present tense:

> We do experiments in science class.
> > (Experiments are usually done in science class.)

> We have science class five days a week.
> > (Science class happens every day.)

Use **past tense** for something that took place in the past.

Examples of past tense:

> The students were in science class yesterday.
> > (Students are no longer in class.)

> We completed our experiment before lunch.
> > (The experiment is done.)

Here are some examples of irregular present tense and past tense verbs.

Present	Past
begin	began
fly	flew
break	broke
bend	bent
cling	clung
do	did
drink	drank
dive	dove or dived

Name: _____ Date: _____

Chapter VI: Learning to Use Present and Past Tense in Science Writing (cont.)

Identifying Present and Past Tense Verbs

Directions: In each sentence below, there is an underlined verb. Check **present** or **past** to show the tense of the underlined verb.

1. Whooping cranes <u>fly</u> from Texas to Canada each summer.   ___ present   ___ past

2. The whooping cranes <u>flew</u> south to Texas last week.   ___ present   ___ past

3. Monarch butterflies <u>cling</u> to the milkweed when laying eggs. ___ present   ___ past

4. A monarch <u>clung</u> to the milkweed for many hours.   ___ present   ___ past

5. The mother whale <u>dove</u> deep into the ocean.   ___ present   ___ past

6. Everyone enjoys watching as the whales <u>dive</u> deep in the
    ocean for food.   ___ present   ___ past

7. The ray of white light <u>bends</u> as it enters the prism.   ___ present   ___ past

8. The ray of white light <u>bent</u>, and we saw the spectrum of
    colors.   ___ present   ___ past

9. A hummingbird <u>hangs</u> in the air as it drinks nectar from
    the flower.   ___ present   ___ past

10. The hummingbird's wings fluttered rapidly as it <u>hung</u> in
    the air.   ___ present   ___ past

Name: _____ Date: _____

Chapter VII: Using Present Tense for Observation; Using Past Tense for Summary

Present Tense

When observing and writing what is taking place in an experiment, scientists use present tense. They are writing down what is happening as they observe the experiment being performed.

Recording Bailey's Seesaw Experiment

Bailey is in science class doing an experiment. Chloe observes Bailey and writes the following description of Bailey's actions as she completes the experiment. Read Chloe's description as Bailey does her experiment. Help Chloe write her description in present tense. The verbs in parentheses are present and past tense. Choose the present tense verb for each sentence and write it on the blanks below. The tenses are in random order, so read the choices carefully.

1. Bailey a) (is/was) working in science class completing her seesaw experiment. She b) (has/had) a ruler, fulcrum, paper, pencil, and pennies on her table. Bailey c) (places/placed) the ruler on the fulcrum at the 6-inch mark. The arms of the ruler d) (were/are) equal. Bailey e) (placed/places) 1 penny at the 3-inch mark. She f) (places/placed) another penny at the 9-inch mark on the ruler. Bailey g) (wrote/writes) down that the ruler balances without adding pennies to either arm of the ruler. Bailey h) (moves/moved) the ruler so the fulcrum i) (was/is) at the 5-inch mark on the ruler. She j) (is/was) recording that it is necessary to place 1 more penny on the penny at the 3-inch mark to balance the ruler. Bailey k) (moves/moved) the ruler so the fulcrum is at the 4-inch mark on the ruler. She l) (is/was) recording that it is necessary to place 1 more penny on the two pennies at the 3-inch mark to balance the ruler.

   a) _____   b) _____   c) _____

   d) _____   e) _____   f) _____

   g) _____   h) _____   i) _____

   j) _____   k) _____   l) _____

   Bailey then draws diagrams of the ruler and fulcrum setups.
   A.   B.   C.

Chapter VII: Using Present Tense for Observation; Using Past Tense for Summary (cont.)

Recording Bailey's Seesaw Experiment (cont.)

Bailey makes a table and records the results for each fulcrum placement.

Balancing Ruler Arms		
Fulcrum under ruler at	Number of pennies at 3″	Number of pennies at 9″
6 inches	1	1
5 inches	2	1
4 inches	3	1

2. Use Bailey's table above to answer the following questions. Circle the number of the correct answer.

   a. As the distance from the fulcrum increased, the single penny would balance

      1) a greater number of pennies.   2) a smaller number of pennies.

   b. As the distance from the fulcrum to the load of pennies decreased, the number of pennies needed to balance the single penny   1) increased.   2) decreased.

3. Bailey wrote the following brief explanation for the results shown in her chart. Help Chloe make sure Bailey's explanation is written in present tense. Complete the blanks by selecting the correct verb from the list below.

   a) want/wanted   b) did/does   c) is/was   d) shows/showed
   e) became/becomes   f) is/was   g) is/was   h) add/added

   I a) _____ you to note that the number of pennies at 9 inches

   b) _____ not increase. The number c) _____ always 1 penny.

   My chart d) _____ that as the length of the resistance arm

   e) _____ shorter, the number of pennies to balance the seesaw

   f) _____ increased. For each inch the resistance arm g) _____

   shortened, I h) _____ more pennies to balance the ruler.

Name: _____ Date: _____

Chapter VII: Using Present Tense for Observation; Using Past Tense for Summary (cont.)

Past Tense

When writing about a completed science experiment, scientists are writing a summary. They are writing to explain what they did in completing the experiment. The experiment was completed in the past. Therefore, a summary is written in past tense.

Summarizing Bailey's Seesaw Experiment

Bailey wrote the following summary report to present to her science class. The report should be written in past tense.

Directions: The verbs in Bailey's summary have been underlined. Help Bailey make sure the summary is written in past tense. If the verb is not in past tense, write the past tense version of the verb on the correct blank below the summary.

Present Tense	Past Tense
complete	completed
need	needed
place	placed
write	wrote
move	moved
record	recorded
move	moved
find	found

For my science experiment I 1) <u>completed</u> a see-saw experiment. The tools I 2) <u>need</u> were a ruler, fulcrum, paper, pencil, and pennies. First, I 3) <u>place</u> the ruler on the fulcrum at the 6-inch mark. The arms of the ruler were equal. I then 4) <u>placed</u> 1 penny at the 3-inch mark and another penny at the 9-inch mark on the ruler. I 5) <u>write</u> in my notes that the ruler balanced without adding pennies to the 3-inch mark or the 9-inch mark. I next 6) <u>moved</u> the ruler so the fulcrum was at the 5-inch mark on the ruler. I then 7) <u>record</u> in my notes that it was necessary to place 1 more penny on the penny at the 3-inch mark to balance the ruler. I then 8) <u>move</u> the ruler so the fulcrum was under the 4-inch mark on the ruler. I 9) <u>found</u> that it was necessary to place 1 more penny on the two pennies at the 3-inch mark to balance the ruler.

1) _____ 2) _____ 3) _____

4) _____ 5) _____ 6) _____

7) _____ 8) _____ 9) _____

Name: _____ Date: _____

Chapter VIII: Writing Explanations and Descriptions

In science class you must often prepare and present an explanation or description for your science projects. When you complete the explanation or description, your teacher will expect you to write sentences that are to the point. Your teacher will also expect you to be able to use present tense and past tense correctly.

Writing Sentences That Make a Single Point in Present Tense

Makhi and Danny were reading about electromagnets in science class. One of the pictures showed an electromagnet made with a battery, copper wire, a nail, and a switch.

Their question: How can the electromagnet be made more powerful?

After reading about electromagnets, they developed the following explanation, or hypothesis.

Hypothesis: Increasing the number of coils of copper wire wound around the nail increases the electromagnet's strength.

Variable to test hypothesis: Number of coils of copper wire wound around iron core (nail)

1. Makhi will write the following description of the electromagnet experiment he and Danny intend to complete to test their hypothesis. Make sure Makhi writes using present tense.

    Complete the blanks using the correct verbs below. Help Makhi make sure the description is written in present tense. Choose carefully, as the tenses are not always in the same order.

    a) is/was   b) wanted/want   c) have/had   d) used/use
    e) was/is   f) want/wanted   g) wind/wound   h) checked/check
    i) increase/increased   j) is/was   k) becomes/became
    l) increased/increases   m) picks/picked   n) plan/planned

    Our experiment a) _____ about electromagnets, which are often used in construction. We b) _____ to find out how the electromagnet can be made stronger. I c) _____ copper wire, a nail, a battery, paper clips, and a switch, which we d) _____ to control the flow of electricity through the copper wire. The variable e) _____ the number of coils we wind around the nail. We f) _____ to find out if the number of paper clips the electromagnet will pick up increases with more coils of wire. To begin, we g) _____ two coils around the nail. Then we h) _____ to see how many paper clips the electromagnet

Chapter VIII: Writing Explanations and Descriptions (cont.)

Writing Sentences That Make a Single Point in Present Tense (cont.)

will pick up. We i) _____ the number of coils around the nail by one coil each time before we check to see how many paper clips the electromagnet will pick up. If our hypothesis j) _____ correct, the electromagnet k) _____ stronger as the number of coils around the iron core l) _____, which we will know is true if the electromagnet m) _____ up more paper clips. We n) _____ to use the following chart to record the experiment data.

Number of coils around nail	Predicted number of paper clips picked up
2	1
3	1
4	2
5	2
6	3
7	3
8	4

Chapter VIII: Writing Explanations and Descriptions (cont.)

Writing Sentences That Make a Single Point in Present Tense (cont.)

2. Reread Makhi's description. Underline the sentences that make a single point. Write the sentences that make more than one point on the blanks below. Make sure each sentence is written in present tense.

Sentences That Make More Than One Point

a. _____
_____

b. _____
_____
_____

c. _____
_____
_____

d. _____
_____
_____

3. Help Makhi rewrite the sentences above for his science writing journal with sentences that make a single point. You may need to break the sentences up into two or more sentences.

a. _____
_____
_____

b. _____
_____
_____

c. _____
_____
_____

d. _____
_____
_____

Name: _____ Date: _____

Chapter VIII: Writing Explanations and Descriptions (cont.)

Writing the Experiment Design and Results in Past Tense

Wentric and Makhi had a science assignment to complete an experiment. While watching a television show about the environment, they heard that compact fluorescent lightbulbs were much better for the environment than incandescent lightbulbs. Wentric and Makhi wondered if compact fluorescent lightbulbs really did use less energy and last much longer. They had the following question.

Their Question: Do compact fluorescent lightbulbs last longer and use less energy than incandescent lightbulbs?

Wentric and Makhi decided that they would perform an experiment to see if the compact fluorescent lightbulbs did last longer and use less energy. They decided on an explanation, or hypothesis, for the experiment.

Their Hypothesis: Compact fluorescent lightbulbs last longer and are more energy efficient than incandescent lightbulbs.

1. After completing their experiment, Wentric and Makhi were preparing to present the experiment design and results to their class. Help Wentric and Makhi write the Experiment Design in past tense. Select past tense verbs from the following verbs to complete the blanks. The verbs presented are in random order as to tense, so choose the verbs carefully.

   a) were/are   b) are/were   c) burned/burn   d) is/was

   e) is/was   f) were/are

Experiment Design

A compact fluorescent lightbulb and incandescent lightbulb a) _____ compared. The two lightbulbs b) _____ compared for light life and energy used. The compact fluorescent lightbulb and the incandescent lightbulb c) _____ for 24 hours per day, 7 days per week. A daily record d) _____ kept that showed the number of hours each lightbulb lasted before the light burned out. The amount of energy used to light each lightbulb e) _____ computed. A graph and written summary f) _____ completed showing the results of the experiment.

Name: _____ Date: _____

Chapter VIII: Writing Explanations and Descriptions (cont.)

Writing the Experiment Design and Results in Past Tense (cont.)

2. Wentric and Makhi then presented a list of tools they used to complete the experiment. Help Wentric and Makhi write the tools presentation in past tense. Circle the past tense verb to complete each blank. The verbs presented are in random order as to tense, so choose the verbs carefully.

Tools Used to Complete Experiment

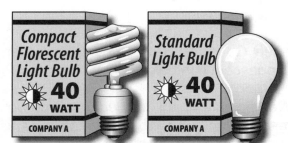

   We a) (purchased/purchase) a 40-watt compact fluorescent lightbulb and a 40-watt incandescent lightbulb. We b) (purchase/purchased) paper and pencil to record the results. We c) (decide/decided) to use graph paper to illustrate the results. We d) (secured/secure) a set of energy costs showing costs for watts/kilowatts used. We e) (purchased/purchase) two identical lamps so our hypothesis could be f) (tests/tested).

3. Makhi and Wentric then presented a graph to the class.

Graph Results

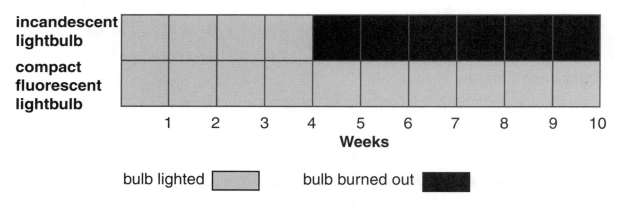

Name: _____ Date: _____

Chapter VIII: Writing Explanations and Descriptions (cont.)

Writing the Experiment Design and Results in Past Tense (cont.)

Writing the Graph Summary

4. Wentric and Makhi wrote the following sentences for their graph summary. The present-tense verbs they used have been underlined. Help them correct the sentences so all the verbs are in past tense. Complete the blanks below to correct the underlined verbs.

   a. Each light <u>is</u> turned on for 24 hours every day, so 7 • 24 = 168 hours per week.

   b. The incandescent lightbulb <u>glows</u> for 672 hours before it burned out.

   c. The incandescent lightbulb <u>uses</u> 40 watts per hour, or 960 watts per 24 hours.

   d. The compact fluorescent lightbulb <u>burns</u> 10 watts per hour, or 240 watts per 24 hours.

   e. The compact fluorescent lightbulb <u>continues</u> to glow until the end of the 10-week experiment.

   f. The energy charge was $0.08 per kilowatt hour, so the compact fluorescent lightbulb <u>saves</u> money over the incandescent lightbulb.

   g. The compact fluorescent lightbulb <u>use</u> fewer watts per hour and glowed much longer.

   h. The compact fluorescent lightbulb <u>is</u> much more efficient.

   i. Our experiment <u>proves</u> that our hypothesis was correct.

   a) _____   b) _____   c) _____

   d) _____   e) _____   f) _____

   g) _____   h) _____   i) _____

Name: _____ Date: _____

Chapter VIII: Writing Explanations and Descriptions (cont.)

Writing Your Experiment Design

Directions: Choose one of the topics from page 10 for which you have already developed a question and hypothesis. In the space below, write an experiment design that you could use to test the hypothesis. Remember to write the experiment design in past tense.

_____

_____

_____

_____

_____

_____

_____

_____

_____

_____

_____

_____

_____

_____

_____

_____

_____

_____

_____

_____

_____

_____

_____

_____

_____

_____

Name: _____ Date: _____

Chapter IX: Writing in Science Using Active and Passive Voice

Active Voice/Passive Voice

When writing in science, you should think: What do I want to emphasize? In science, writing in the active voice is usually more effective than writing in the passive voice. In **active voice**, the subject does the acting. In **passive voice**, the subject receives the action. Writing science information in active voice gives stronger emphasis than passive voice. In active voice, the subject does the acting. Active voice makes it easier to write sentences that make a clear point. In passive voice, the subject is the receiver of the action.

Active Example: In the sentence below, Tommy and Chloe are the subject. Tommy and Chloe are emphasized. They do the acting.

Tommy and Chloe completed the experiment.

Passive Example: The sentence below is in passive voice. The experiment is emphasized. Experiment is the subject. Tommy and Chloe are the actors but not the subject.

The experiment was completed by Tommy and Chloe.

Writing in Active Voice

Directions: In each sentence below, determine if the sentence is written in active or passive voice. Place a check on the blank that shows the voice of the verb in the sentence. Underline the subject in each sentence.

1. Lexus wrote her science experiment in class.   ____ active   ____ passive

2. The experiment was written by Lexus in class.   ____ active   ____ passive

3. Five paper clips were picked up by the magnet.   ____ active   ____ passive

4. The magnet picked up five paper clips.   ____ active   ____ passive

5. Wentric used a copper wire to connect the batteries.   ____ active   ____ passive

6. A copper wire was used by Wentric to connect the batteries. ____ active   ____ passive

7. Makhi placed wax on the board to reduce the friction. ____ active   ____ passive

8. Wax was placed on the board by Makhi to reduce friction. ____ active   ____ passive

9. Danny watched the bees collect pollen.   ____ active   ____ passive

10. The bees collecting pollen were watched by Danny.   ____ active   ____ passive

Name: _____ Date: _____

Chapter IX: Writing in Science Using Active and Passive Voice (cont.)

Writing About Experiments in Active Voice

Tommy and Chloe completed the following experiments.

Experiment 1: Static Electricity

1. Complete the blanks for Experiment 1 using the words below. Some words will be used more than once. Then, answer the questions that follow.

    Tommy's   They   Tommy   He   Chloe   Each   She

    a) _____ and Chloe were studying static electricity and electrons.
    b) _____ wanted to find out more about static electricity. c) _____
    of them selected an experiment. d) _____ decided he would rub a balloon
    with his wool cap. e) _____ placed the balloon on the wall to see if the
    balloon would stick to the wall. f) _____ rubbed a plastic rod with Tommy's
    wool hat. g) _____ held the plastic rod near Tommy's head. h) _____
    hair stood up like a bad hair day. i) _____ thought the wool hat was rubbing
    electrons off the balloon and plastic rod.

2. In sentence a), the subject is _____ and Chloe. _____ and Chloe
    are the actors. The sentence is in the (active/passive) voice.

3. In sentence b), the subject is _____. _____ and _____
    are the actors. The sentence is in the (active/passive) voice.

4. In sentence c), the subject is _____. _____ and _____
    are the actors. The sentence is in the (active/passive) voice.

5. In sentence d), the subject is _____. _____ is the actor. The sen-
    tence is in the (active/passive) voice.

6. In sentence e), the subject is _____. _____ is the actor. The sen-
    tence is in the (active/passive) voice.

7. In sentence f), the subject is _____. _____ is the actor. The sen-
    tence is in the (active/passive) voice.

8. In sentence g), the subject is _____. _____ is the actor. The sen-
    tence is in the (active/passive) voice.

9. In sentence h), the subject is _____. _____ is the actor.
    The sentence is in the (active/passive) voice.

10. In sentence i), the subject is _____. _____ is the actor. The sen-
    tence is in the (active/passive) voice.

Name: _____ Date: _____

Chapter IX: Writing in Science Using Active and Passive Voice (cont.)

Writing About Experiments in Active Voice (cont.)

Experiment 2: Static Electricity

1. Complete the blanks for Experiment 2 using the words below. Some words will be used more than once. Then, answer the questions that follow.

   balloon   hat   experiment   hair   wool   rod

   a) A static electricity _____ was completed by Tommy and Chloe.
   b) A wool hat and a _____ were used by Tommy to complete his experiment. c) The _____ was rubbed with the wool hat by Tommy. d) The _____ was placed on the wall by Tommy. e) A plastic _____ and a wool _____ were used by Chloe to complete her experiment. f) The plastic _____ was rubbed with the wool hat by Chloe. g) The plastic _____ was placed near Tommy's hair by Chloe. h) The _____ strands on Tommy's head were caused to stand up by the plastic rod.

2. In sentence a), the subject is _____. The _____ receives the action. The sentence is in the (active/passive) voice.

3. In sentence b), the subject is _____ and _____.
   _____ and _____ receive the action. The sentence is in the (active/passive) voice.

4. In sentence c), the subject is _____. The _____ receives the action. The sentence is in the (active/passive) voice.

5. In sentence d), the subject is _____. The _____ receives the action. The sentence is in the (active/passive) voice.

6. In sentence e), the subject is _____ and _____.
   The _____ and _____ receive the action. The sentence is in the (active/passive) voice.

7. In sentence f), the subject is _____. The _____ receives the action. The sentence is in the (active/passive) voice.

8. In sentence g), the subject is _____. The _____ receives the action. The sentence is in the (active/passive) voice.

9. In sentence h), the subject is _____. The _____ receives the action. The sentence is in the (active/passive) voice.

Name: _____ Date: _____

Chapter IX: Writing in Science Using Active and Passive Voice (cont.)

Rewriting Sentences in the Active Voice

Directions: Rewrite each sentence to change the verb from passive voice to active voice.

1. The rust experiment was completed by Lexus and Bailey.

   _____

   _____

2. The experiment was used by Lexus and Bailey to prove that rust is a chemical action.

   _____

   _____

3. An experiment using a prism was completed by Makhi and Danny.

   _____

   _____

4. The iron bar was heated by Tommy and Lexus.

   _____

   _____

5. A magnet was used by Chloe to pick up the paper clips.

   _____

   _____

6. The first Law of Motion was stated by Isaac Newton.

   _____

   _____

7. Fluorescent and incandescent lightbulbs were used by Makhi for his experiment.

   _____

   _____

8. The electromagnet was made stronger by Danny.

   _____

   _____

Name: _____   Date: _____

Chapter X: Verb Tense; Active or Passive Voice

Using the Correct Verb Tense and Voice When Reporting About Experiments

Hummingbirds and Flowers

Lexus and Chloe are watching hummingbirds. The hummingbirds are hanging in the air while sipping nectar from the flower blossoms. The flowers have large red, white, and yellow blossoms. The flowers are all growing in flower pots.

Lexus says, "Chloe, I have been watching the hummingbirds, and I wonder which flower the hummingbirds like best."

Chloe answers, "I think the hummingbirds like the red flower best."

They decided to do an experiment to see if they could find an answer. They knew that they must develop an explanation, or hypothesis, for their experiment. They also knew their hypothesis must be stated so they could identify the variable to test.

Lexus Describes Her Experiment

Lexus's hypothesis: Hummingbirds are not attracted to one color of flower more than others.

Lexus's variable: Three potted flower plants each with one of the colors red, yellow, or white

Directions: Lexus's experiment description must be presented to her science class. Lexus wrote the following sentences as she prepared a description of her experiment. Read each sentence and complete the blanks for verb tense and voice.

1. I am observing hummingbirds for my experiment.

    Verb tense: ____ present   ____ past   Voice: ____ active   ____ passive

2. The hummingbirds are observed by me one hour each day for nine days.

    Verb tense: ____ present   ____ past   Voice: ____ active   ____ passive

3. I made the one-hour observation of the hummingbirds at 2:00 P.M. each day.

    Verb tense: ____ present   ____ past   Voice: ____ active   ____ passive

4. I recorded each time a hummingbird chose a given flower color.

    Verb tense: ____ present   ____ past   Voice: ____ active   ____ passive

Name: _____   Date: _____

Chapter X: Verb Tense; Active or Passive Voice (cont.)

Lexus Describes Her Experiment (cont.)

5. A record of the hummingbird choices is made by me.

    Verb tense: ____ present   ____ past   Voice: ____ active   ____ passive

6. I selected the following tools for my experiment.

    Verb tense: ____ present   ____ past   Voice: ____ active   ____ passive

7. Three potted flowers (each pot has one of the colors red, yellow, or white), a pencil, paper, and a clock are my tools.

    Verb tense: ____ present   ____ past   Voice: ____ active   ____ passive

8. I place the flower pots in a line one foot apart.

    Verb tense: ____ present   ____ past   Voice: ____ active   ____ passive

9. I rotated the flower pots from right to left each day before making my observation.

    Verb tense: ____ present   ____ past   Voice: ____ active   ____ passive

10. The flower color placements are made randomly by me.

    Verb tense: ____ present   ____ past   Voice: ____ active   ____ passive

11. The colors red, yellow, and white are written on pieces of paper by me.

    Verb tense: ____ present   ____ past   Voice: ____ active   ____ passive

12. The three pieces of paper were placed in a paper sack by me.

    Verb tense: ____ present   ____ past   Voice: ____ active   ____ passive

13. The pieces of paper with color names are drawn out one at a time by Chloe.

    Verb tense: ____ present   ____ past   Voice: ____ active   ____ passive

14. I make a bar graph to show the results of my experiment.

    Verb tense: ____ present   ____ past   Voice: ____ active   ____ passive

Name: _____   Date: _____

Chapter X: Verb Tense; Active or Passive Voice (cont.)

Rewriting Lexus's Experiment Description in Past Tense as a Summary

Lexus's teacher looked at her experiment description. The teacher told her that for her science report, she must write the summary of her experiment in past tense.

Directions: For each blank, choose the past tense verb and help Lexus rewrite her experiment description as a summary using past tense. The verbs presented are in random order as to tense, so choose the verbs carefully.

1) choose/chose   2) observe/observed   3) make/made   4) recorded/record

5) was/is   6) select/selected   7) were/are   8) placed/place

9) rotate/rotated   10) are/was   11) are/were   12) were/are

13) are/was   14) made/make

I 1) _____ hummingbirds for my experiment. The hummingbirds were 2) _____ by me one hour each day for nine days. I 3) _____ the one-hour observation at 2:00 P.M. each day. I 4) _____ each time a hummingbird chose a given flower color. A record of the hummingbird choices 5) _____ made by me. I 6) _____ the following tools for my experiment. Three potted flowers (each pot had one of the colors red, yellow, or white), a pencil, paper, and a clock 7) _____ my tools. I 8) _____ the flower pots in a line one foot apart. I 9) _____ the flower pots from right to left each day before making my observation. The flower color placement 10) _____ made randomly. The colors red, yellow, and white 11) _____ written on pieces of paper by me. The three pieces of paper 12) _____ placed in a paper sack by me. Each piece of paper with color names 13) _____ drawn out one at a time by Chloe. I 14) _____ a bar graph to show the results of my experiment.

Name: _____ Date: _____

Chapter X: Verb Tense; Active or Passive Voice (cont.)

Rewriting Lexus's Experiment Description in Active Voice

The following sentences in Lexus's summary are in passive voice. Lexus's teacher told her that passive sentences were helpful in making the report flow better, but she should not overuse passive sentences. Lexus should rewrite the sentences using active voice. Then she can determine if her report is stronger with the sentences rewritten in active voice.

Directions: Help Lexus rewrite the following sentences from her experiment description in active voice.

1. The hummingbirds were observed by me one hour each day for nine days.

   I _____

   _____

2. A record of the hummingbird choices was made by me.

   I _____

   _____

3. Three potted flowers (each pot had one of the colors red, yellow, or white), a pencil, paper, and a clock were my tools.

   My _____

   _____

   _____

4. The colors red, yellow, and white were written on pieces of paper by me.

   I _____

   _____,_____

5. The three pieces of paper were placed in a paper sack by me.

   I _____

   _____

6. Each piece of paper with the color names was drawn out one at a time by Chloe.

   Chloe _____

   _____

7. While Lexus does not have to change any of the sentences to active voice if she doesn't want to, read the sentences and see what you think. Write the numbers of the sentences that you would change from passive to active voice for her report on the lines below.

   _____ _____ _____ _____ _____ _____

Name: _____ Date: _____

Chapter X: Verb Tense; Active or Passive Voice (cont.)

Chloe Describes Her Experiment

Chloe's Hypothesis: Red flowers attract more hummingbirds than white or yellow flowers.

Chloe's Variables: Three potted flower plants in the colors red, yellow, and white

Directions: Chloe wrote the following sentences as a guide to help her when writing her experiment report. Lexus pointed out to Chloe that when writing in science, she should omit, or leave out, sentences that do not have anything to do with completing the experiment. Read the sentences and place a check (✓) on the Omit blank if Chloe's sentence does not have anything to do with the experiment. These sentences should be left out of her class report. For the sentences that Chloe should use in her report, complete the blanks for the tense and voice of the sentence.

1. I think hummingbirds are very pretty.

    ____ Omit   Verb tense: ____ present ____ past   Voice: ____ active ____ passive

2. I found it was fun to observe the hummingbirds sipping nectar.

    ____ Omit   Verb tense: ____ present ____ past   Voice: ____ active ____ passive

3. The hummingbirds were observed by me for two 1/2-hour periods a day for nine days.

    ____ Omit   Verb tense: ____ present ____ past   Voice: ____ active ____ passive

4. I make a half-hour observation at 10:00 A.M. and 2:00 P.M. each day.

    ____ Omit   Verb tense: ____ present ____ past   Voice: ____ active ____ passive

5. I count the hummingbirds sipping nectar from different-colored flowers.

    ____ Omit   Verb tense: ____ present ____ past   Voice: ____ active ____ passive

6. I sure hope it is sunny and warm each day.

    ____ Omit   Verb tense: ____ present ____ past   Voice: ____ active ____ passive

7. I would hate to wear a jacket while completing my experiment.

    ____ Omit   Verb tense: ____ present ____ past   Voice: ____ active ____ passive

Name: _____ Date: _____

Chapter X: Verb Tense; Active or Passive Voice (cont.)

Chloe Describes Her Experiment (cont.)

8. Three potted flowers, one each of red, yellow, and white flowers; paper; pencil; and a clock were chosen by me as the tools to use.

    ____ Omit   Verb tense: ____ present   ____ past   Voice: ____ active   ____ passive

9. I really like the flower color purple.

    ____ Omit   Verb tense: ____ present   ____ past   Voice: ____ active   ____ passive

10. A pot of flowers is placed out by me each day.

    ____ Omit   Verb tense: ____ present   ____ past   Voice: ____ active   ____ passive

11. I use the same color flower each day at 10:00 A.M. and 2:00 P.M.

    ____ Omit   Verb tense: ____ present   ____ past   Voice: ____ active   ____ passive

12. I placed each flower color before the hummingbirds for a three-day period.

    ____ Omit   Verb tense: ____ present   ____ past   Voice: ____ active   ____ passive

13. I placed another flower color before the hummingbirds for the second three-day period.

    ____ Omit   Verb tense: ____ present   ____ past   Voice: ____ active   ____ passive

14. I place the third color flower out for the third three-day period.

    ____ Omit   Verb tense: ____ present   ____ past   Voice: ____ active   ____ passive

15. My favorite flower color is yellow.

    ____ Omit   Verb tense: ____ present   ____ past   Voice: ____ active   ____ passive

16. That is why I have my yellow skirt on today.

    ____ Omit   Verb tense: ____ present   ____ past   Voice: ____ active   ____ passive

17. I do not want any bias in my experiment.

    ____ Omit   Verb tense: ____ present   ____ past   Voice: ____ active   ____ passive

18. I decided the order of presenting the flowers must be random.

    ____ Omit   Verb tense: ____ present   ____ past   Voice: ____ active   ____ passive

Name: _____   Date: _____

Chapter X: Verb Tense; Active or Passive Voice (cont.)

Chloe Describes Her Experiment (cont.)

19. To determine the flower order, I placed the names of the colors on three pieces of paper.
    ___ Omit   Verb tense: ___ present   ___ past   Voice: ___ active   ___ passive

20. Lexus draws the pieces of paper out one at a time.
    ___ Omit   Verb tense: ___ present   ___ past   Voice: ___ active   ___ passive

21. The first color drawn was placed out by me for the first three days.
    ___ Omit   Verb tense: ___ present   ___ past   Voice: ___ active   ___ passive

22. I place the second color out for the second three days.
    ___ Omit   Verb tense: ___ present   ___ past   Voice: ___ active   ___ passive

23. Then I placed the third color before the hummingbirds the last three days.
    ___ Omit   Verb tense: ___ present   ___ past   Voice: ___ active   ___ passive

24. I think I will have lots of fun doing this experiment.
    ___ Omit   Verb tense: ___ present   ___ past   Voice: ___ active   ___ passive

25. How many of you think this is a "cool" experiment?
    ___ Omit   Verb tense: ___ present   ___ past   Voice: ___ active   ___ passive

26. I graph the results of my experiment.
    ___ Omit   Verb tense: ___ present   ___ past   Voice: ___ active   ___ passive

27. Write the numbers of the sentences that should not be in Chloe's science report.

    _____   _____   _____   _____   _____   _____

Name: _____   Date: _____

Chapter X: Verb Tense; Active or Passive Voice (cont.)

Rewriting Chloe's Experiment Description in Past Tense as a Summary

Chloe's teacher looked at her sentences and told her that the summary for her science report must be written in past tense.

Directions: Help Chloe rewrite her experiment description using past tense. Draw a line to mark out the present tense verb choice in each pair. This will leave Chloe with only the past tense verbs.

The hummingbirds were (observed/observe) by me for two ½-hour periods a day for nine days. I (make/made) a half-hour observation at 10:00 A.M. and 2:00 P.M. each day. I (observe/observed) the hummingbirds sipping nectar from different-colored flowers. Three potted red, yellow, and white flowers; paper; pencil; and a clock were (select/selected) by me as the tools to use. A pot of flowers (was/is) placed out by me each day. The pots (were/is) set out each day at 10:00 A.M. and 2:00 P.M. A flower color (is/was) placed before the hummingbirds for a three-day period. Then for the second three days I (place/placed) another flower color before the hummingbirds. The third color flower (replace/replaced) the second color for a three-day period. I (do/did) not want any bias in my experiment. So I (know/knew) I must randomly determine the order of presenting the flowers. To determine the flower order, I (placed/place) the names of the colors on three pieces of paper. Lexus (draws/drew) the pieces of paper out one at a time. The first color (was/is) placed out for the first three days. The second color (is/was) set out for the second three days. I (place/placed) the third color before the hummingbirds the last three days. I (made/make) a graph to show the results of my experiment.

Chapter X: Verb Tense; Active or Passive Voice (cont.)

Rewriting Chloe's Experiment Description in Active Voice

Chloe's teacher told her passive sentences were helpful in making the report flow better. For example, it provides an alternative to beginning every sentence with the word *I*. However, passive voice should not be overused. To make sure she was not overusing passive voice, Chloe should rewrite the sentences using active voice. Then she can determine if her report would be stronger with the sentences written in active voice.

Directions: Help Chloe rewrite the following sentences from her experiment description in active voice.

1. The hummingbirds were observed by me for two 1/2-hour periods a day for nine days.

    I _____

    _____

2. Three potted red, yellow, and white flowers; paper; pencil; and a clock were chosen by me as the tools to use.

    I _____

    _____

3. A pot of flowers was placed out by me each day.

    I _____

    _____

4. The pots were set out each day at 10:00 A.M. and 2:00 P.M.

    I _____

    _____

5. A flower color was placed before the hummingbirds for a three-day period.

    I _____

    _____

6. The first color was placed out for the first three days.

    I _____

    _____

7. The second color was set out for the second three days.

    I _____

    _____

8. Chloe does not have to change any of the sentences in her report from passive voice to active voice. However, if you think she should change the sentence to active voice in the report, write the number of the sentence on one of the blanks below.

    _____   _____   _____   _____   _____   _____   _____

Name: _____ Date: _____

Chapter X: Verb Tense; Active or Passive Voice (cont.)

Writing Your Own Experiment Summary

Directions: Use the experiment design you wrote on page 26, and assume you have conducted the experiment. Write a summary of your experiment on the lines below. Remember to use the past tense. Also use a balance of active and passive voice so your writing flows naturally.

_____

_____

_____

_____

_____

_____

_____

_____

_____

_____

_____

_____

_____

_____

_____

_____

_____

_____

_____

_____

_____

Name: _____   Date: _____

Chapter XI: Writing the Science Summary

Writing Makhi and Danny's Summary in Past Tense

Makhi and Danny completed their experiment. They developed tables to show their predicted results and actual results. Table I below shows their predicted results before the experiment. Table II shows the actual results after completing the experiment. Danny's summary of Table I is written below.

Summary of Predicted Results From Table I

Directions: Read the summary and complete the blanks using the verbs below to help Danny write the summary in the past tense. The tenses in each pair may vary from present/past to past/present, so read the choices carefully.

1) began/begin
2) predicted/predict
3) increase/increased
4) predict/predicted
5) picked/pick
6) increase/increased
7) was/is
8) is/was
9) think/thought
10) increased/increase

When we 1) _____ the experiment, we made the predictions in Table I. We 2) _____ that as we 3) _____ the number of coils around the nail, the strength of the electromagnet would increase. We 4) _____ that the number of paper clips 5) _____ up would be 6) _____ by the numbers in the table. It 7) _____ our prediction that the number of paper clips picked up 8) _____ related to a specific number of coils. We 9) _____ that for every two coils, the number of paper clips picked up would be 10) _____ by one clip.

Table I

Number of coils around nail	Predicted number of paper clips picked up
2	1
3	1
4	2
5	2
6	3
7	3
8	4

Name: _____ Date: _____

Chapter XI: Writing the Science Summary (cont.)

Summary of Actual Results From Table II

Directions: Danny's summary of Table II is written below. Read the summary and complete the blanks to help Danny write the summary in the past tense. The tenses in each pair may vary from present/past to past/present, so read the choices carefully.

1) compile/compiled
2) compared/compare
3) is/was
4) do/did
5) predict/predicted
6) was/is
7) predict/predicted
8) become/became
9) became/become
10) begin/began
11) picked/pick
12) increase/increased
13) predict/predicted

After we 1) _____ our results following the experiment, we 2) _____ Table I and Table II. In Table I and Table II as the coils of wire increased, there 3) _____ a relationship between number of coils of wire and the electromagnet strength. The increased strength of the electromagnet 4) _____ not work out exactly as we had 5) _____. The number of coils and paper clips relationship 6) _____ as we 7) _____ until the number of coils 8) _____ greater than five coils. As the number of coils 9) _____ greater than five, the strength of the electromagnet 10) _____ to increase. The number of paper clips 11) _____ up 12) _____ at a rate greater than we had 13) _____.

Table II

Number of coils around nail	Actual number of paper clips picked up
2	1
3	1
4	2
5	2
6	3
7	4
8	5
9	7

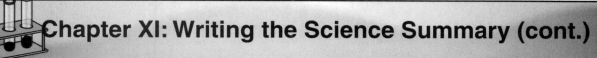

Chapter XI: Writing the Science Summary (cont.)

Writing Lexus's Summary in Past Tense and Active Voice

Lexus had completed her science experiment on electromagnets. Her science teacher assigned her to make a summary report of her experiment. Lexus had to explain her experiment. Then she had to write a summary of the results of the experiment.

Lexus's Explanation

Lexus wrote the following explanation for her summary report. Help Lexus make sure her report is written in past tense. The tenses in each pair may vary from present/past to past/present, so read the choices carefully.

1) connected/connect
2) wound/wind
3) connect/connected
4) flowed/flows
5) wind/wound
6) picked/pick
7) wind/wound
8) wound/wind
9) pick/picked
10) continue/continued
11) wind/wound
12) check/checked
13) picks/picked
14) disconnect/disconnected
15) wound/wind
16) connect/connected
17) check/checked

I 1) _____ the wire to one post of the battery. Then I 2) _____ the wire around the nail one time. I then 3) _____ the free end of the wire to the other battery post. Now an electrical current 4) _____ through the wire. The nail with the wire 5) _____ around it is an electromagnet. The electromagnet 6) _____ up one paper clip. I then 7) _____ the wire around the nail two times. The nail with the wire 8) _____ around it two times 9) _____ up two paper clips. I 10) _____ the steps until the wire had been 11) _____ around the nail ten times. Each time, I 12) _____ to see if the nail 13) _____ up more paper clips. Each time I 14) _____ the wire connected to the battery and let the paper clips fall. Then after I 15) _____ the wire around the nail, I 16) _____ the wire to the battery. Then I again 17) _____ to see if the electromagnet would pick up more paper clips.

Name: _____ Date: _____

Chapter XI: Writing the Science Summary (cont.)

Lexus's Summary

Lexus used the table below to prepare her summary report. She knew that she must make sure the class understood her table. Lexus wrote the following sentences to help her write the summary. Help Lexus make sure her sentences are written in past tense and active voice. Use the verbs below to complete the blanks. The tenses in each pair may vary from present/past to past/present, so read the choices carefully.

Table I

Coils of wire around nail	1	2	3	4	5	6	7	8	9	10
Grams the nail picked up	0.25	0.5	0.75	1	1	1.5	1.75	2	2.25	2.5

a) is/was b) begin/began c) wind/wound

d) increased/increase e) were/is f) is/was

g) used/use h) increase/increased i) is/were

j) is/was k) is/were l) picked/picks

m) add/added n) is/was o) picked/picks

p) was/is q) is/was r) was/is

s) is/was t) increase/increased

1. Table I a) _____ developed by me to summarize the results of my experiment.

2. My experiment b) _____ as I c) _____ one coil of wire around the nail and attempted to pick up a paper clip.

3. After each attempt to pick up paper clips, I d) _____ coils by one until ten coils e) _____ on the nail.

4. The strength of the electromagnet f) _____ measured by me in grams.

5. I g) _____ grams because each paper clip weighed 0.25 gram.

6. I h) _____ the grams amount to be picked up by 0.25 gram for each new coil.

7. In Table I, as the first three coils i) _____ added by me, an additional 0.25 gram j) _____ picked up for each coil.

8. When four coils k) _____ added by me, the electromagnet l) _____ up one gram.

Name: _____ Date: _____

Chapter XI: Writing the Science Summary (cont.)

Lexus's Summary (cont.)

9. When I m) _____ coil five, the electromagnet strength n) _____ not increased.

10. The electromagnet o) _____ up an extra 0.5 gram, or two paper clips, when coil six p) _____ added by me.

11. After coil six q) _____ added by me, the increase in grams picked up r) _____ 0.25 gram, or one paper clip, per added coil.

12. In the experiment, the strength of the electromagnet s) _____ increased as the number of coils around the nail t) _____.

13. The sentences written in passive voice are ____, ____, ____, ____, ____, and ____.

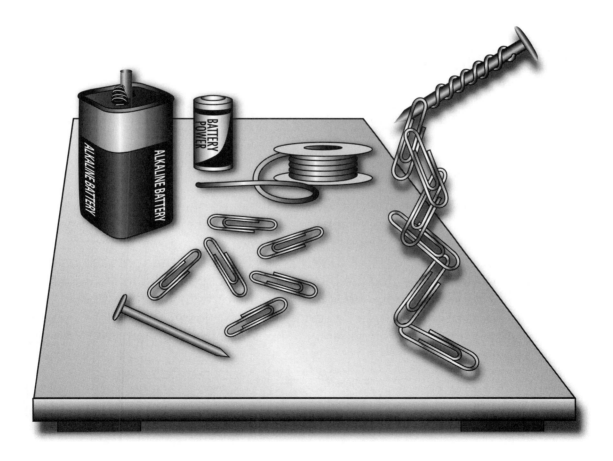

Name: _____   Date: _____

Chapter XI: Writing the Science Summary (cont.)

Selecting the Best Written Summary of an Experiment

When writing the summary of a science experiment, you want the reader to understand the experiment. Therefore, you must write very clearly. Steer away from wordy explanations unless it is necessary to understand the experiment.

Directions: Read each pair of summaries for science experiments carefully. Then select the summary from each pair that was written with only the facts needed so a reader could easily understand the summary.

Summaries A and B

Summary A: Yesterday we decided to do an experiment that would be fun and not take very long. We walked to the ice cream shop and ordered a malt. I had chocolate and my friend had vanilla. We talked about our experiment while we drank our malts. The malt was delicious, but mine was a little more than I wanted. We decided to do an experiment about electricity. This experiment was chosen by us to find out how to make an electrical circuit. To complete the experiment, we need a battery with two posts, two pieces of copper wire, a lightbulb with a socket, and a switch. It took us quite a while to find the tools for the experiment. We were getting tired, so we decided to meet the next day to complete the experiment. We hope that our experiment will prove that our hypothesis is correct. We watched a movie before going to bed.

Summary B: Our experiment was to make electricity flow through an electrical circuit and make a lightbulb glow.

Our hypothesis was: Electricity only flows through a closed electrical circuit.

We needed a 3-volt battery with two posts, two 1-foot pieces of insulated copper wire, a light-bulb in a socket with two posts, and a switch for our experiment. First, we stripped 1⁄2 inch of insulation from each end of the two pieces of copper wire. Second, we connected one end of each wire to the posts on the battery. Third, we connected one of the wires to one post of the lightbulb socket. Fourth, we connected the other end of the copper wire to the switch. Fifth, we connected the other copper wire from the lightbulb to the other pole of the switch. The switch was open, so the electrical circuit was not complete. We closed the switch, and the light-bulb glowed. An electrical circuit was completed. The lightbulb began to glow. The experiment proved our hypothesis.

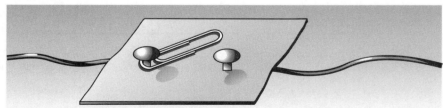

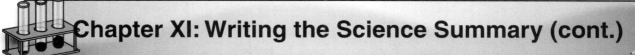

Chapter XI: Writing the Science Summary (cont.)

Summaries A and B (cont.)

Directions: Complete the blanks to compare Summary A and Summary B. Place the letter of the summary that has that characteristic on the blank in the sentence. Then check the characteristics that made it easier to understand a summary.

_____ 1. In Summary _____, sentences were shorter and to the point.

_____ 2. In Summary _____, sentences were written in active voice.

_____ 3. In Summary _____, sentences were written in the same tense.

_____ 4. In Summary _____, the sentences were clear and easy to understand.

_____ 5. In Summary _____, there were sentences that had nothing to do with the experiment.

_____ 6. In Summary _____, the hypothesis was stated and confirmed or rejected.

Summaries C and D

Summary C: Our hypothesis was that fish could be trained using a specific signal. We designed an experiment to train the fish. We placed five different-colored goldfish in an aquarium. We divided the aquarium front into quadrants. Our goal was to train the fish to come to the upper right quadrant to feed. We used the following procedure to complete our experiment. Just before feeding, we made two light taps against the glass in the upper right quadrant. After 5 seconds, we dropped fish food into the upper right quadrant. The training period was for 14 days with the taps made at different times each day. We recorded the seconds it took for the fish to respond to the two taps and swim to the upper right quadrant to feed. We averaged the seconds each day. The average response time ranged from 16.8 seconds on Day 1 to 3.8 seconds on Day 14.

The experiment proved our hypothesis that fish could be trained to come to a specific location to feed.

Chart I

Day #

	1	2	3	4	5	6	7	8	9	10	11	12	13	14
Fish a	17	18	16	15	13	14	12	10	8	6	6	4	3	2
Fish b	18	16	16	14	13	10	9	9	8	7	8	5	5	3
Fish c	10	14	13	13	12	11	10	8	7	6	9	6	5	4
Fish d	19	18	18	16	15	13	10	12	10	9	7	6	5	4
Fish e	20	18	19	18	18	15	13	11	10	8	9	7	7	6

Average Response Time (seconds)

Name: _____ Date: _____

Chapter XI: Writing the Science Summary (cont.)

Summary D: In class, we were watching the goldfish swimming in an aquarium. Someone said, "Hey, I have a great idea! Let's try to train the goldfish." Our hypothesis was that fish could be trained to come to a specific location in an aquarium. An experiment was designed to see if fish could be trained. Five different-colored goldfish are placed in an aquarium. The fish are just absolutely beautiful. They all were so brightly colored. They swam around all day as though they were playing. We enjoyed watching them. The aquarium front was divided into quadrants. The goal was to train the fish to come to the upper right quadrant to feed. Just before feeding,

two light taps were made against the glass in the upper right quadrant. After 5 seconds, fish food was dropped into the upper right quadrant. The training period was for 20 days with the taps made at different times each day. A record was made of the fish that responded to the two taps by swimming to the upper right quadrant.

Directions: Complete the blanks to compare Summary C and Summary D. Place the letter of the summary that has that characteristic on the blank in the sentence. Then check the characteristics that made it easier to understand a summary.

_____ 1. In Summary _____, sentences were shorter and to the point.

_____ 2. In Summary _____, sentences were written in active voice.

_____ 3. In Summary _____, sentences were all in the same tense.

_____ 4. In Summary _____, the sentences were clear and easy to understand.

_____ 5. In Summary _____, there were sentences that had nothing to do with the experiment.

_____ 6. In Summary _____, the chart made it easier to understand the experiment.

_____ 7. In Summary _____, the hypothesis was stated and confirmed or rejected.

Name: _____ Date: _____

Chapter XII: Explanations Using Graphs, Charts, and Diagrams

Including Charts, Graphs, or Diagrams in Experiments

In science, an explanation of graphs, charts, and diagrams is often a part of the class assignment. Before presenting an explanation, the main parts of the graph, chart, or diagram must be determined.

Rocket Graph

In science, Tommy's class was studying rockets. The parabola below shows the travel range of a launched rocket. Height and distance are in kilometers. The rocket was launched at 10:00 A.M., and it landed at 11:00 A.M. Tommy's assignment was to write an explanation of the information presented on the graph. He was to write the explanation so it could be read and understood by students who had missed class. Help Tommy write his explanation.

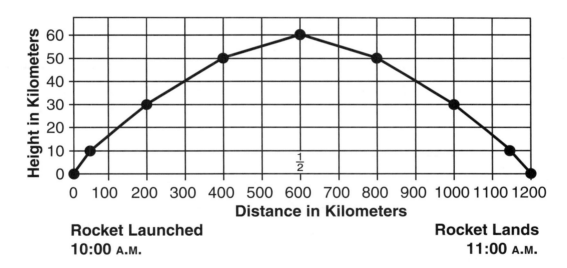

Rocket Launched
10:00 A.M.

Rocket Lands
11:00 A.M.

Preparing to Write the Explanation

1. What data is shown on the graph about distance?

    _____

    _____

    _____

    _____

Chapter XII: Explanations Using Graphs, Charts, and Diagrams (cont.)

Rocket Graph (cont.)

2. What does the data show about height?

    _____

    _____

    _____

3. What does the data show about the rocket launch time?

    _____

    _____

4. What does the data show about the rocket landing time?

    _____

    _____

5. What does the data show about the rocket flight time?

    _____

    _____

6. Write an explanation for the above graph to be placed in Tommy's science writing journal. Write complete sentences that make a single point, are in present tense, and use active voice.

    _____

    _____

    _____

    _____

    _____

    _____

    _____

    _____

    _____

    _____

    _____

Name: _____ Date: _____

Chapter XII: Explanations Using Graphs, Charts, and Diagrams (cont.)

Earth/Sun Diagram

Danny was in Earth Science class. The teacher was using the diagram below for the students to figure out why seasons come and go on Earth. Danny studied the diagram and saw that the Northern Hemisphere has summer when the earth is farthest from the sun. He asked his teacher why this was true. His teacher told Danny to write down his question. Then he should make a hypothesis that he thought would answer his question. She told him that many times the answer to a hypothesis is found by analyzing graphs, charts, or diagrams. She told him to study the diagram below and determine the main points made in the diagram. Understanding Diagram I would help him find the answer to his question and determine if his hypothesis was true or false.

Diagram I

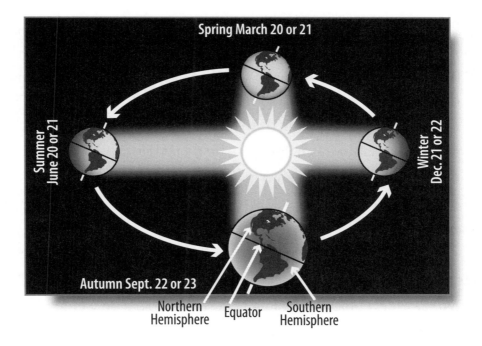

Danny's Question: Why does the Northern Hemisphere have summer when the earth is farthest from the sun?

Danny's Hypothesis: The earth's North Pole axis is tilted toward the sun in summer, so the Northern Hemisphere receives more hours of daylight for each 24-hour period.

Name: _____   Date: _____

Chapter XII: Explanations Using Graphs, Charts, and Diagrams (cont.)

Earth/Sun Diagram (cont.)

Danny used Diagram I and made the statements below. His teacher told him to check his statements carefully to make sure they were true. Help Danny review his statements before he makes his explanation and determines what Diagram I tells him about his hypothesis.

Preparing to Write the Explanation

Directions: Place the letter "T" on the blank if Danny's statement is true.

_____ 1. The oval shows the orbit of the earth around the sun

_____ 2. The earth is shown moving around the sun in a clockwise direction.

_____ 3. The earth is shown moving around the sun in a counterclockwise direction.

_____ 4. The sun is shown as the white circle with the earth rotating around the sun.

_____ 5. The sun is shown as the white circle rotating around the earth.

_____ 6. The earth is closer to the sun in the Northern Hemisphere summer than in winter.

_____ 7. The earth is closer to the sun in the Northern Hemisphere winter than in summer.

_____ 8. The earth's axis is shown with a white vertical line.

_____ 9. The earth's axis is shown with a white slanting line.

_____ 10. The earth's axis is always pointing in the same direction during the orbit.

_____ 11. The earth's North Pole axis always points toward the sun.

_____ 12. The earth's North Pole axis points toward the sun in the Northern Hemisphere summer.

_____ 13. The earth's North Pole axis points toward the sun in the Northern Hemisphere winter.

_____ 14. The earth's North Pole axis points away from the sun in winter.

_____ 15. It takes the earth one year to make a complete orbit around the sun.

_____ 16. It takes the earth more than one year to complete one orbit around the sun.

_____ 17. During one complete orbit around the sun, the earth has four seasons.

_____ 18. Each season is approximately three months long.

_____ 19. Some seasons are much longer than others.

_____ 20. The seasons in order are summer, fall, winter, and spring.

_____ 21. The seasons in order are summer, spring, winter, and fall.

Name: _____ Date: _____

Earth/Sun Diagram (cont.)

22. Use Danny's true statements for the Earth/Sun diagram and help Danny write an explanation for his science writing journal. Select the order of the sentences that make it easiest to understand the diagram. Write sentences that make a single point, are in present tense, and use active voice.

_____

_____

_____

_____

_____

_____

_____

_____

_____

_____

_____

_____

_____

_____

Name: _____   Date: _____

Chapter XII: Explanations Using Graphs, Charts, and Diagrams (cont.)

Interpreting Charts

Tommy and Lexus are studying whales, fish, and dinosaurs in science class. Their assignment for class is to research a certain species of whale, fish, and dinosaur to see if there are similarities among the three species. Using their research, they must write an explanation to be presented orally to their class. The explanation must tell what they found out in their research about whale, fish, and dinosaur species. The explanation must not take more than ten minutes. To help them prepare their explanation and stay within the ten-minute limit, they developed the list of characteristics below. They developed a rectangular chart titled Characteristics Chart to record the characteristics of the whale, fish, and dinosaur species they chose. The completed Characteristics Chart shows a plus sign (+) in the rectangle if the animal has the characteristic.

Characteristics

a. lays eggs   b. gives birth to live young   c. lives on land
d. lives in water   e. has lungs   f. has gills
g. reptile   h. mammal   i. fish
j. migrates   k. herbivore   l. extinct
m. weight in tons   n. warm-blooded   o. cold-blooded

Characteristics Chart

Animal	a	b	c	d	e	f	g	h	i	j	k	l	m	n	o
Clown fish	+			+		+			+						+
Humpback whale		+		+	+			+		+			+	+	
Stegosaur	+		+		+		+				+	+	+		+

Directions: Help Tommy and Lexus use the Characteristics Chart to develop their explanation. Tommy and Lexus wrote the following ten sentences as they prepared their explanation. Complete the blanks on the checklist below each sentence to help Tommy and Lexus make sure the sentences make a single point, are in active voice, and use the correct verb tense. The sentences about clown fish and humpback whales should be written in the present tense. The sentences about stegosaurs should be written in the past tense. The general statements about the research should be in past tense.

1. We made the chart to compare the characteristics of clown fish, humpback whales, and stegosaurs.

____ Single point ____ Active Voice ____ Passive Voice ____ Present Tense ____ Past Tense

2. Clown fish are members of the fish family, and humpback whales are mammals.

____ Single point ____ Active Voice ____ Passive Voice ____ Present Tense ____ Past Tense

Name: _____ Date: _____

Chapter XII: Explanations Using Graphs, Charts, and Diagrams (cont.)

Interpreting Charts (cont.)

3.   Stegosaurs are reptiles.

____ Single point   ____ Active Voice   ____ Passive Voice   ____ Present Tense   ____ Past Tense

4.   The chart compared clown fish, humpback whales, and stegosaurs on 15 characteristics.

____ Single point   ____ Active Voice   ____ Passive Voice   ____ Present Tense   ____ Past Tense

5.   Clown fish lay eggs, and stegosaurs also laid eggs.

____ Single point   ____ Active Voice   ____ Passive Voice   ____ Present Tense   ____ Past Tense

6.   Clown fish and humpback whales are alike on the chart because they both lived in water.

____ Single point   ____ Active Voice   ____ Passive Voice   ____ Present Tense   ____ Past Tense

7.   Humpback whales had lungs, and stegosaurs had lungs when they lived on earth.

____ Single point   ____ Active Voice   ____ Passive Voice   ____ Present Tense   ____ Past Tense

8.   Humpback whales weigh tons, and stegosaurs also weighed tons.

____ Single point   ____ Active Voice   ____ Passive Voice   ____ Present Tense   ____ Past Tense

9.   Clown fish are cold-blooded, and stegosaurs were also cold-blooded.

____ Single point   ____ Active Voice   ____ Passive Voice   ____ Present Tense   ____ Past Tense

10.   We found clown fish, humpback whales, and stegosaurs unalike on all of the other characteristics in the chart.

____ Single point   ____ Active Voice   ____ Passive Voice   ____ Present Tense   ____ Past Tense

11.   The chart made by us did not show any one characteristic alike for clown fish, humpback whales, and stegosaurs.

____ Single point   ____ Active Voice   ____ Passive Voice   ____ Present Tense   ____ Past Tense

Name: _____ Date: _____

Chapter XII: Explanations Using Graphs, Charts, and Diagrams (cont.)

Interpreting Charts (cont.)

Directions: Place the numbers of the sentences that Tommy and Lexus must rewrite on the blanks below. Place the letters "pv" on the blank following the sentence number if the sentence is in passive voice and must be rewritten in active voice. Place the letter "t" on the blank if a verb in the sentence is in the wrong tense. Place the letter "p" on the blank if the sentence makes more than one point.

Sentence #	Voice	Tense	More than One Point
_____	_____	_____	_____
_____	_____	_____	_____
_____	_____	_____	_____
_____	_____	_____	_____
_____	_____	_____	_____

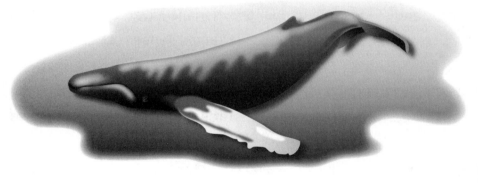

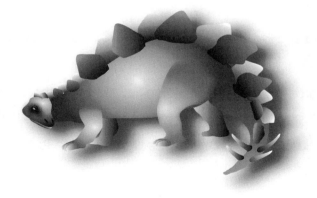

Name: _____   Date: _____

Chapter XIII: Using Coordinating Conjunctions to Combine Sentences

Knowing What Coordinating Conjunctions Mean

In science writing, you must first think about making sentences to the point. However, there are times when you will want to join two sentences to make your writing sound more natural and give it variety. Then you will use a coordinating conjunction. The coordinating conjunction that you use to join sentences must be chosen carefully. To use coordinating conjunctions properly, you must know the meaning of the conjunction.

Coordinating Conjunctions: and, but, for, or, nor, yet, so

Meaning When Used as Coordinating Conjunction:
   a. and: addition, also, too
   b. but: unless, though, nevertheless, whether, on the contrary
   c. for: because, that, since, in view of the fact, for as much
   d. or: alternate explanation
   e. nor: not, neither
   f. yet: nevertheless, notwithstanding
   g. so: with the result that, in order that

Joining Sentences Using Coordinating Conjunctions

Directions: The pairs of sentences below may be joined using a coordinating conjunction. Two conjunctions are given from which you can choose. Write on the blank the coordinating conjunction you would choose to join the two sentences. Also, write the letter for the meaning of the chosen conjunction on the blank provided.

1. Ice is a solid. Ice will float.

    but   nor   Conjunction: _____   Meaning: _____

2. Heat travels from hot to cold. An ice cube gains heat from the surrounding warmer water.

    or   so   Conjunction: _____   Meaning: _____

3. The earth's crust is made up of large plates. When the plates bump against each other, large mountains may be formed.

    but   so   Conjunction: _____   Meaning: _____

Chapter XIII: Using Coordinating Conjunctions to Combine Sentences (cont.)

Joining Sentences Using Coordinating Conjunctions (cont.)

4. An electric circuit may be made using a battery, copper wire, a switch, and a lightbulb. When the switch is open, electrons cannot flow through the electric circuit.

   or   but   Conjunction: _____   Meaning: _____

5. Gravity is a downward force on an object in water. A cork will float because the upward force of buoyancy is greater than the weight of the cork.

   or   yet   Conjunction: _____   Meaning: _____

6. Density is how closely the atoms are packed in an object. A Styrofoam ball and plastic ball do not have the density of a bowling ball.

   so   nor   Conjunction: _____   Meaning: _____

7. The smaller the circumference of a copper wire, the less easily the electrons flow through the wire. The larger the circumference, the more easily the electrons flow through a copper wire.

   nor   and   Conjunction: _____   Meaning: _____

8. When two lightbulbs are on in a series circuit, if one light goes out, neither light will glow. When two lightbulbs are on parallel circuits, if one light goes out, the other light will still glow.

   but   and   Conjunction: _____   Meaning: _____

9. Light waves bend when they enter water. The speed of the wave changes when going from the air to the water.

   for   but   Conjunction: _____   Meaning: _____

10. When a light ray strikes a flat surface, the rays are reflected at the angle the ray hits the surface. When light rays hit the flat surface of a quiet lake, the rays are reflected at the angle the ray hit the lake surface.

    but   so   Conjunction: _____   Meaning: _____

Name: _____ Date: _____

Chapter XIII: Using Coordinating Conjunctions to Combine Sentences (cont.)

Explaining a False Hypothesis

Danny wondered why summer begins on June 21 and winter on December 21 in the Northern Hemisphere. His hypothesis was: Summer begins on June 21 in the Northern Hemisphere because the earth is closer to the sun on that date, and winter begins on December 21 because the earth is farther from the sun.

After research and reading about the seasons, Danny found that his hypothesis was incorrect. Danny must prepare a report for his science class explaining why his hypothesis was incorrect.

Directions: Read through Danny's explanation once. Then help Danny correct his explanation to make sure the underlined verbs are in present tense by completing the first exercise. Next, help Danny correctly use coordinating conjunctions to connect sentences in the explanation.

Danny Explains His False Hypothesis

My hypothesis states that the earth <u>was</u> closer to the sun in summer. (A) That hypothesis is false. I <u>wanted</u> to use Diagram I to explain why my hypothesis <u>was</u> false. Using Diagram I, I <u>could</u> explain why the first day of summer in the Northern Hemisphere <u>was</u> June 21. (B) Diagram I also <u>helped</u> me explain why the first day of winter is on December 21. In the Northern Hemisphere, June 21 is the first day of summer. (C) This is the year's longest daylight period for any 24-hour period. The first day of winter <u>came</u> on December 21. This is the year's shortest daylight period for any 24-hour period. The tilt of the earth's axis <u>was</u> used to explain summer and winter in the Northern Hemisphere. The earth's axis is tilted 23 1/2°. (D) I <u>found</u> the tilt of the axis <u>was</u> the key factor when explaining summer and winter in the Northern Hemisphere. The diagram <u>showed</u> that the northern axis of the earth on June 21 <u>pointed</u> toward the sun. On December 21, the northern axis of the earth <u>pointed</u> away from the sun. (E) The Northern Hemisphere <u>received</u> less daylight and more darkness in each 24-hour period in the winter. It <u>was</u> the tilt of the earth's axis toward the sun that <u>determined</u> why the Northern Hemisphere summer <u>began</u> on June 21. The earth is farthest from the sun on this date. (F) The Northern Hemisphere is tilted toward the sun. The Northern Hemisphere <u>received</u> more daylight during the summer. The tilt of the Northern Hemisphere axis <u>was</u> away from the sun when winter comes on December 21. (G) The earth <u>was</u> closer to the sun on this date than on June 21. (H) The Northern Hemisphere <u>received</u> less daylight during the winter. This <u>meant</u> the Northern Hemisphere <u>was</u> colder during the winter even though the earth <u>was</u> closer to the sun than during the summer.

Name: _____ Date: _____

Chapter XIII: Using Coordinating Conjunctions to Combine Sentences (cont.)

Danny Explains His False Hypothesis (cont.)

Diagram I

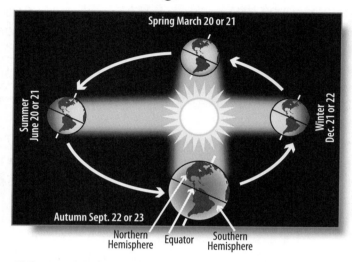

Helping Danny Correct His Explanation

1. Reread Danny's report. Change the underlined verbs in his explanation from past tense to present tense on the blanks below.

Past Tense	Present Tense	Past Tense	Present Tense
a. was	_____	m. pointed	_____
b. wanted	_____	n. received	_____
c. was	_____	o. was	_____
d. could	_____	p. determined	_____
e. was	_____	q. began	_____
f. helped	_____	r. received	_____
g. came	_____	s. was	_____
h. was	_____	t. was	_____
i. found	_____	u. received	_____
j. was	_____	v. meant	_____
k. showed	_____	w. was	_____
l. pointed	_____	x. was	_____

Name: _____   Date: _____

Chapter XIII: Using Coordinating Conjunctions to Combine Sentences (cont.)

Helping Danny Correct His Explanation (cont.)

2. Help Danny use coordinating conjunctions to connect some of the sentences in his explanation. Conjunction locations are shown with capital letters. The conjunction will connect the sentences located before and after the capital letter. Use the coordinating conjunctions **so, and, yet, but,** and **for** to replace the capital letters. Make sure the conjunction used has the correct meaning.

Coordinating Conjunctions Meanings:

and: addition, also, too

but: unless, though, nevertheless, whether, on the contrary

for: because, that, since, in view of the fact, for as much

yet: nevertheless, notwithstanding

so: with the result that, in order that

A. _____

B. _____

C. _____

D. _____

E. _____

F. _____

G. _____

H. _____

Name: _____ Date: _____

Chapter XIV: Writing a Science Report

*Format for a Science Report

A science report is often written to be kept for others to use as a reference. In that case, the report must follow a specific format. There are different formats, but most reports contain the following basic information. Your teacher will have specific guidelines for writing your science report.

Wentric and Makhi's teacher wants them to write a science report for their lightbulb experiment. Their teacher suggested they follow the basic format below in writing their report.

1. **Title Page:** This is page 1 and should be a separate page.
2. **Introduction:** This begins on page 2.
3. **Method:** This section follows the Introduction.
4. **Results:** This section continues after the Method section.
5. **Discussion:** This section continues after the Results section.
6. **Bibliography:** If your teacher requires one, this should be on a separate page.
7. **Appendices:** Use as many appendices as needed. Start each appendix on a new page. Label each appendix as Appendix A, Appendix B, and so on.

Other important format information:
- Number each page of the report. Put the page number in the upper right-hand corner of the page.
- Staple all pages together.
- Use a 12-point standard font, such as Times, Geneva, or Helvetica.
- Double space text on 8 1/2" by 11" paper with one-inch margins, single sided.
- Indent the first line of each paragraph.

Sample of What Your Report Should Look Like (Length of each section will vary.)

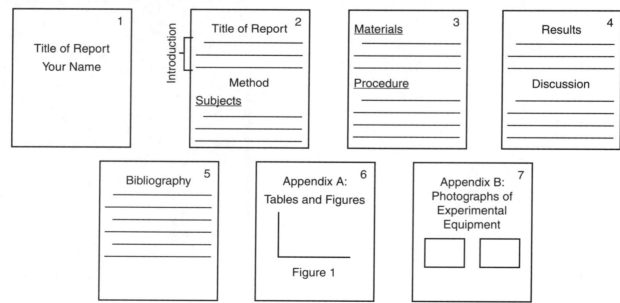

*Reprinted with permission from *Science Writing* by David W. and Ruth Ann Wilson. Mark Twain Media, Inc., Publishers. 1997.

Name: _____ Date: _____

Chapter XIV: Writing a Science Report (cont.)

Title Page

1. On a **Title Page**, include your name and the title of your report. Give your paper a specific title that tells what you did in your research project. For example, a title like *The Effects of Color on Hummingbird Feeding Preference* is more informative and specific than a title like *Feeding Hummingbirds*.

    • The title page for Wentric and Makhi's experiment says:

*Comparing the Light Life and Energy Efficiency of Compact Fluorescent
Lightbulbs and Incandescent Lightbulbs*
Authors:
Wentric Williams and Makhi Lewis

Introduction

2. In the **Introduction**, give the reader the necessary background for understanding your experiment.

    • Start this section on a new page.

    • Center the title of the report at the top of this page, too.

    • Do NOT put the word *Introduction* on this page. It is implied that this section is the introduction—you don't have to say so.

    • By the end of the Introduction, the reader should have a clear understanding of (1) why you are doing this study; (2) how your study fits in with what is already known about the topic; and (3) what you expect to find.

    Directions: A good introduction contains the following information. Help Wentric and Makhi write the introduction in present tense by circling the present tense verb in each sample sentence.

    a. General statements about the topic being studied:

        1. There (are / were) many different kinds of lightbulbs available today.

    b. The specific problem identified on this research project:

        2. Compact fluorescent lightbulbs (were / are) advertised as being better for the environment.

Name: _____ Date: _____

Chapter XIV: Writing a Science Report (cont.)

Introduction (cont.)

3. However, compact fluorescent lightbulbs (did / do) cost more than incandescent lightbulbs.

c. A question that follows from that problem:

4. (Do / did) compact fluorescent lightbulbs last longer and use less energy than incandescent lightbulbs?

d. Past research or other information that helps the reader with context to understand your research:

5. Today, energy (is / was) very expensive.

6. People (are / were) looking for ways to save money.

7. They also (wanted / want) to protect the environment.

8. Manufacturers (claimed / claim) that compact fluorescent lightbulbs last for up to five years.

9. They (were / are) also supposed to use less energy than incandescent bulbs.

Directions: Help Makhi and Wentric select and circle the past tense verb for each sentence in the statement of purpose and hypothesis part of the Introduction.

e. A statement of the purpose of your research:

10. The first purpose of this research (is / was) to see if compact fluorescent lightbulbs lasted longer than incandescent lightbulbs.

11. The second purpose (was / is) to examine the energy usage of compact fluorescent lightbulbs compared to incandescent lightbulbs.

f. The hypothesis for your study:

12. It (is / was) hypothesized that compact fluorescent lightbulbs last longer and are more energy efficient than incandescent lightbulbs.

Name: _____ Date: _____

Chapter XIV: Writing a Science Report (cont.)

Method

3. In the **Method** section, tell the reader exactly how you carried out the research—that is, how you tested the hypothesis. The Methods sections should be written in past tense.

   • Begin this section with the following centered heading—Method

   • Continue from where the Introduction finished.

   • Describe your study in enough detail that someone else could do the same study just like you did it.

   • Within the Method section, include appropriate subsections such as the following:

   a. Subjects

   b. Materials

   c. Procedure

   Place each of the subheadings at the left-hand margin of the page (see illustration). The appropriate content for each of the subsections is described below.

   a. <u>Subjects</u>: Describe what or who you studied—whether it was animals, humans, rocks, plants, or the weather. Be specific.

   Directions: Wentric and Makhi's Subject section might look like this. Answer the following questions about their Subject section.

   We compared two kinds of lightbulbs both manufactured by Company A. The first lightbulb was a 40-watt compact fluorescent bulb that cost $6.25. The second lightbulb was a 40-watt incandescent bulb that cost $1.15.

   1. What wattage were the lightbulbs equivalent to? _____

   2. What company manufactured the lightbulbs? _____

   3. How much did the compact fluorescent lightbulb cost? _____

   4. How much did the incandescent lightbulb cost? _____

Chapter XIV: Writing a Science Report (cont.)

Method (cont.)

b. <u>Materials</u>: Describe all the materials used in the study—whether equipment, stimuli to which subjects were exposed, or other items necessary in carrying out the research procedures.

Directions: Wentric and Makhi's Materials section might look like this. Answer the following questions about their Materials section.

Each lightbulb was screwed into one of a matched set of lamps. Both lamps used a toggle switch to complete the circuit. Both lamps were plugged into the same electrical outlet. Matching lamp shades were attached to each lightbulb.

1. What type of switch did each lamp have? _____

2. Where did the lamps get their electricity? _____

3. Were the lamps different in any way? _____

c. <u>Procedure</u>: Describe what was done and when. Give the reader a step-by-step description of what you did. Pretend you are telling a story: Start at the beginning and don't stop until you have explained the very last thing you did in carrying out your research.

Directions: Wentric and Makhi's Procedure section might look like this. Answer the following questions about their Procedure section.

Each bulb was purchased new at the same time. The bulbs were screwed into their designated lamps and each lamp was plugged in at the same time. The lamp shades were attached. At exactly the same time, both lamps were switched on (4:30 in the evening on Wednesday).

The lights were left on 24 hours a day, seven days a week. Each bulb was checked at 6:30 A.M.; 4:30 P.M.; and 9 P.M. every day. Each day and week both bulbs remained lit was charted. When the incandescent lightbulb burned out, the time and date was recorded, and the lamp was unplugged. At the end of the ten weeks allotted for the experiment, the total amount of hours of light for each bulb was tallied.

Name: _____ Date: _____

Chapter XIV: Writing a Science Report (cont.)

Method (cont.)

Using a set of energy costs for watts/kilowatts used obtained from the electric company, the total cost of operation for each bulb was computed. The incandescent lightbulb was lit for 672 hours before it burned out. The incandescent light used 40 watts per hour. The total watts used was 672 • 40 = 26,880. The energy charge was $0.08 per kilowatt-hour. The watts were divided by 1,000 to get the kilowatt-hours (26,880 ÷ 1,000 = 26.88). The kilowatt-hours were then multiplied by 0.08 to get the total energy charge (26.88 • $0.08 = $2.1504). The energy charge for the compact fluorescent lightbulb for the same 672 hours was then computed. The compact fluorescent lightbulb puts out the same amount of light as a 40-watt incandescent lightbulb, but it only uses 10 watts per hour. To figure the energy usage for the compact fluorescent lightbulb, the hours were multiplied by the watts (672 • 10 = 6,720), the watts were divided by 1,000 to get the kilowatt-hours (6,720 ÷ 1,000 = 6.72), and the kilowatt-hours were multiplied by the energy charge (6.72 • $0.08 = $0.5376).

1. At what time were the lamps switched on? _____

2. How many hours did the incandescent lightbulb burn? _____

3. What was the total energy charge for the hours that the incandescent lightbulb burned? _____

4. What was the total energy charge for the same hours for the compact fluorescent lightbulb? _____

5. Did Wentric and Makhi use present tense or past tense verbs for their Method section? _____

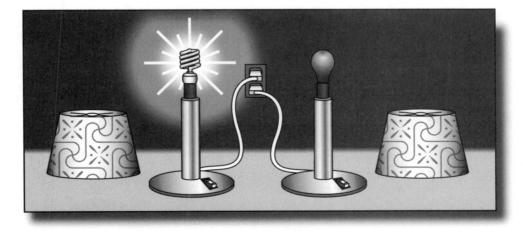

Name: _____ Date: _____

Chapter XIV: Writing a Science Report (cont.)

Results

4. In the **Results** section, tell the reader what you found.

*   Begin this section with the centered heading—Results. Just continue from where the Method section finished.

*   Make sure the reader can tell from the results whether or not the hypothesis was supported.

*   Summarize your findings. Of course, you should tell the reader in words what you found. However, you might also cite statistics or use tables and figures (graphs) to illustrate your findings.

*   The Results section should be written in past tense.

*   Do not discuss overall conclusions or implications in this section. Save that for the Discussion section.

Directions: Wentric and Makhi's Results section might look like this. Answer the questions that follow about their Results section.

The main finding of the study was that the incandescent bulb burned out after only four weeks, while the compact fluorescent bulb remained lit throughout the entire 10-week experiment. Secondly, the compact fluorescent lightbulb cost less to operate than the incandescent lightbulb. The total energy charge for the incandescent lightbulb was approximately $2.15. For the same 672 hours, the total energy charge for the compact fluorescent lightbulb was approximately $0.54.

The compact fluorescent lightbulb lasted at least 60% longer than the incandescent lightbulb. Figure 1 (see Appendix A) shows how long each lightbulb lasted. Figure 2 (see Appendix C) compares the energy usage of the two lightbulbs. It shows that the compact fluorescent lightbulb cost approximately 75% less to operate than the incandescent lightbulb.

1. How much longer did the compact fluorescent lightbulb last? _____

2. Where can you find the data to answer that question? _____

3. How much less did the compact fluorescent lightbulb cost to operate?

    _____

4. Where can you find the data to answer that question? _____

Name: _____ Date: _____

Chapter XIV: Writing a Science Report (cont.)

Discussion

5. In the **Discussion** section, draw some conclusions and indicate how your research has contributed to a better understanding of the problem under investigation.

    • Begin this section with the centered heading—Discussion. Just continue from where the Results section finished.

    • A good Discussion section progresses in this sequence:

    a. Briefly restate the purpose of the study.

    b. Indicate how the findings relate to your hypothesis. Was your hypothesis supported?

    c. Discuss the meaning of your results. Why did you find what you did?

    d. Discuss possible implications of your research. How does the research help you understand or solve some problem?

    e. Indicate any questions that remain unanswered.

    • Write the Discussion section in past tense.

    Directions: Wentric and Makhi's Discussion section might look like this. Answer the following questions about their Discussion section.

    There were two purposes for this research. One purpose was to compare how long compact fluorescent lightbulbs and incandescent lightbulbs lasted. The second purpose was to compare the energy costs for the two types of lightbulbs.

    Our hypothesis that compact fluorescent lightbulbs last longer and are more energy efficient than incandescent lightbulbs was supported by the research.

    Compact fluorescent bulbs were cheaper to operate than incandescent bulbs. The initial purchase price of the compact fluorescent bulb was higher than the incandescent, but the cost of operating the bulb over the lifespan of the bulb was considerably less. The break-even point for cost was projected to occur in week 12. From that point on, the compact fluorescent bulb would pay for itself.

    If our interpretation of the present findings was correct, we have found that consumers can save money and reduce their energy use by switching all the lightbulbs in their house to compact fluorescent. Schools and businesses can save money as well.

Name: _____ Date: _____

Chapter XIV: Writing a Science Report (cont.)

Discussion (cont.)

One problem with the present research was the limited time frame. Because the incandescent lightbulb did burn out within the ten-week research time frame, the total potential savings of the compact fluorescent lightbulb was not identified. Future research should examine the total lifespan of a compact fluorescent lightbulb.

1. Was Wentric and Makhi's hypothesis supported or not? _____

2. Which lightbulb lasted the longest? _____

3. Which lightbulb cost the most to operate? _____

4. How could Wentric and Makhi improve this experiment to better test their hypothesis? _____

   _____

Bibliography

6. In the **Bibliography** section, list all the sources you consulted in preparing your report.

   • Begin this section on a new page with the following centered heading—Bibliography.

   • In listing the sources, follow a consistent format. Ask your teacher which format you should use.

   Directions: Wentric and Makhi used the website listed below as a source. They included this citation in their bibliography. Answer the following questions about the citation.

   Corand, Matt. (2008). "Kilowatt/Hour Usage Rates." <www.palco-oprates.com> 2008, August 12.

   1. What organization published the information on the website?

      _____

   2. Who is the author of the information? _____

   3. When did Wentric and Makhi access the information? _____

Name: _____ Date: _____

Chapter XIV: Writing a Science Report (cont.)

Appendices

7. Use **Appendices** for (1) all Tables and Figures (graphs) that were referred to in the Results section, and (2) any special material that does not fit well in the main body of the report (for example, a copy of the "Kilowatt/Hour Usage Rates").

   • Begin each appendix on a new page. If you have just one appendix, begin the page with the following centered heading—Appendix. If you have more than one appendix, use the following headings—Appendix A, Appendix B, and so on.

   • Give each appendix an appropriate title. Center the title on the line below the Appendix heading.

   Directions: Wentric and Makhi put the following information in their Appendix section. Answer the questions below about their Appendix section.

Appendix A
Figure 1: Length of Time the Lightbulbs Remained Lighted

Appendix B
Table 1: Kilowatt/Hour Usage Rates

Appendix C
Figure 2: Cost of Energy Usage for Compact Fluorescent and Incandescent Lightbulbs

1. How many pages are in the Appendix section? _____

2. If you wanted to see which lightbulb lasted longer, to which appendix would you turn? _____

3. If you wanted to see which lightbulb was more expensive to operate, to which appendix would you turn? _____

Chapter XIV: Writing a Science Report (cont.)

Writing Your Own Science Report

Use the skills you have learned to write a science report about an experiment you have conducted. In the space below, write your question and your hypothesis.

Question: _____

_____

_____

Hypothesis: _____

_____

_____

Come up with a title for your report and write it below.

_____

_____

Use the rest of the space for notes for getting your report organized. Write the complete report on your own paper. Be sure to follow the guidelines for writing a science report given on pages 62–71. Your teacher may have additional requirements and guidelines for your report.

_____

_____

_____

_____

_____

_____

_____

_____

_____

_____

_____

Answer Keys

Chapter I
Subjects and Predicates (pg. 1)

Subject	Verb
1. A screw	is
2. Velocity	is
3. Water pressure	exerts
4. Weight	may be measured
5. Density	is
6. Volume	measures
7. Static electricity	is
8. An atom	has
9. Protons and neutrons	are found
10. Protons	have

Keeping Subjects and Predicates Close Together (pg. 2)
Answers will vary.

Chapter II
Writing Sentences With One Main Point (pg. 3)
1. one point
2. more than one point
3. one point
4. one point
5. more than one point
6. one point
7. one point
8. one point
9. more than one point
10. one point

Getting Right to the Main Point, Part 1 (pg. 4)
1. a; is
2. d; is
3. e; float
4. h; move
5. i; is made
6. l; separated
7. n; cause
8. p; are
9. r; were formed

Getting Right to the Main Point, Part 2 (pg. 5)
#3 makes the main point.

Getting Right to the Main Point, Part 3 (pg. 5)
The earth's crust is made up of 12 large tectonic plates. These plates float on semi-molten rock. The earth's crust is a few miles thick. The earth's crust is thicker under the continents. The plates move very slowly. The plates separated many years ago. Plate movements cause great changes in the earth's surface. Large mountain chains are often the result of plates bumping together. The Andes Mountains were formed when two plates bumped together.

Chapter III
Developing a Hypothesis to Answer the "Why" Question (pg. 6–7)
1. b 2. c 3. c 4. a 5. c 6. b

Chapter IV
Forming a Hypothesis About Prisms and Refracted Light (pg. 8)
Answers will vary.

Forming a Hypothesis About Electromagnets (pg. 9)
Answers will vary.

Forming Your Own Questions and Hypotheses (pg. 10)
Answers will vary.

Chapter V
Chloe's Die-Tossing Experiment (pg. 11–12)
Answers will vary.

Wentric's Coin-Flipping Experiment (pg. 13–14)
Answers will vary.

Chapter VI
Identifying Present and Past Tense Verbs (pg. 16)
1. present
2. past
3. present
4. past
5. past
6. present
7. present
8. past
9. present
10. past

Chapter VII
Recording Bailey's Seesaw Experiment (pg. 17–18)
1. a. is b. has c. places d. are
   e. places f. places g. writes h. moves
   i. is j. is k. moves l. is
2. a. 1 b. 1
3. a. want b. does c. is d. shows
   e. becomes f. is g. is
   h. add

Summarizing Bailey's Seesaw Experiment (pg. 19)
2. needed 3. placed 5. wrote
7. recorded 8. moved

Chapter VIII
Writing Sentences That Make a Single Point in Present Tense (pg. 20–22)
1. a. is b. want c. have
   d. use e. is f. want
   g. wind h. check i. increase
   j. is k. becomes l. increases
   m. picks n. plan

2. a. Our experiment is about electromagnets, which are often used in construction.
   b. I have copper wire, a nail, a battery, paper clips, and a switch, which we use to control the flow of electricity through the copper wire.
   c. We increase the number of coils around the nail by one coil each time before we check to see how many paper clips the electromagnet will pick up.
   d. If our hypothesis is correct, the electromagnet becomes stronger as the number of coils around the iron core increases, which we will know is true if the electromagnet picks up more paper clips.
3. Answers will vary.

Writing the Experiment Design and Results in Past Tense (pg. 23–25)

1. a. were   b. were   c. burned
   d. was   e. was   f. were
2. a. purchased   b. purchased   c. decided
   d. secured   e. purchased   f. tested
4. a. was   b. glowed   c. used
   d. burned   e. continued   f. saved
   g. used   h. was   i. proved

Chapter IX
Writing in Active Voice (pg. 27)

1. active   Lexus
2. passive   The experiment
3. passive   Five paper clips
4. active   The magnet
5. active   Wentric
6. passive   A copper wire
7. active   Makhi
8. passive   Wax
9. active   Danny
10. passive   The bees collecting pollen

Writing About Experiments in Active Voice
Experiment 1: Static Electricity (pg. 28)

1. a. Tommy   b. They   c. Each
   d. Tommy   e. He   f. Chloe
   g. She   h. Tommy's   i. They
2. Tommy, Tommy, active
3. They, Tommy and Chloe, active
4. Each, Tommy and Chloe, active
5. Tommy, Tommy, active
6. He, Tommy, active
7. Chloe, Chloe, active
8. She, Chloe, active
9. Tommy's hair, Tommy's hair, active
10. Chloe, Chloe, active

Experiment 2: Static Electricity (pg. 29)

1. a. experiment   b. balloon   c. balloon
   d. balloon   e. rod, hat   f. rod
   g. rod   h. hair
2. experiment, experiment, passive
3. hat, balloon, Hat, balloon, passive
4. balloon, balloon, passive
5. balloon, balloon, passive
6. rod, hat, rod, hat, passive
7. rod, rod, passive
8. rod, rod, passive
9. hair, hair, passive

Rewriting Sentences in the Active Voice (pg. 30)

1. Lexus and Bailey completed the rust experiment.
2. Lexus and Bailey used the experiment to prove that rust is a chemical action.
3. Makhi and Danny completed an experiment using a prism.
4. Tommy and Lexus heated the iron bar.
5. Chloe used a magnet to pick up the paper clips.
6. Isaac Newton stated the first Law of Motion.
7. Makhi used fluorescent and incandescent lightbulbs for his experiment.
8. Danny made the electromagnet stronger.

Chapter X
Lexus Describes Her Experiment (pg. 31–32)

1. present   active   2. present   passive
3. past   active   4. past   active
5. present   passive   6. past   active
7. present   passive   8. present   active
9. past   active   10. present   passive
11. present   passive   12. past   passive
13. present   passive   14. present   active

Rewriting Lexus's Experiment Description in Past Tense as a Summary (pg. 33)

1. chose   2. observed   3. made
4. recorded   5. was   6. selected
7. were   8. placed   9. rotated
10. was   11. were   12. were
13. was   14. made

Rewriting Lexus's Experiment Description in Active Voice (pg. 34)

1. I observed the hummingbirds one hour each day for nine days.
2. I made a record of the hummingbird choices.
3. My tools were three potted plants (each pot had one of the colors red, yellow, or white), a pencil, paper, and a clock.
4. I wrote the colors red, yellow, and white on pieces of paper.

5. I placed the three pieces of paper in a paper sack.
6. Chloe drew out each piece of paper with the color names one at a time.
7. Answers will vary.

Chloe Describes Her Experiment (pg. 35–37)

1. Omit			2. Omit	
3. past	passive		4. present	active
5. present	active		6. Omit	
7. Omit			8. past	passive
9. Omit			10. present	passive
11. present	active		12. past	active
13. past	active		14. present	active
15. Omit			16. Omit	
17. present	active		18. past	active
19. past	active		20. present	active
21. past	passive		22. present	active
23. past	active		24. Omit	
25. Omit			26. present	active

27. 1, 2, 6, 7, 9, 15, 16, 24, 25

Rewriting Chloe's Experiment Description in Past Tense as a Summary (pg. 38)

Present tense verbs have been removed.

The hummingbirds were (observed) by me for two 1⁄2-hour periods a day for nine days. I (made) my one-half hour observation at 10:00 A.M. and 2:00 P.M. each day. I (observed) the hummingbirds sipping nectar from different-colored flowers. Three potted red, yellow, and white flowers; paper; pencil; and a clock were (selected) by me as the tools to use. A pot of flowers (was) placed out by me each day. The pots (were) set out each day at 10:00 A.M. and 2:00 P.M. A flower color (was) placed before the hummingbirds for a three-day period. Then for the second three days I (placed) another flower color before the hummingbirds. The third color flower (replaced) the second color for a three-day period. I (did) not want any bias in my experiment. So I (knew) I must randomly determine the order of presenting the flowers. To determine the flower order, I (placed) the names of the colors on three pieces of paper. Lexus (drew) the pieces of paper out one at a time. The first color (was) placed out for the first three days. The second color (was) set out for the second three days. I (placed) the third color before the hummingbirds the last three days. I (made) a graph to show the results of my experiment.

Rewriting Chloe's Experiment Description in Active Voice (pg. 39)

1. I observed the hummingbirds for two 1/2-hour periods a day for nine days.
2. I chose three potted red, yellow, and white flowers; paper; pencil; and a clock as the tools to use.
3. I placed a pot of flowers out each day.

4. I set the pots out each day at 10:00 A.M. and 2:00 P.M.
5. I placed a flower color before the hummingbirds for a three-day period.
6. I placed the first color out for the first three days.
7. I set out the second color for the second three days.
8. Answers will vary.

Chapter XI
Summary of Predicted Results From Table I (pg. 41)

1. began	2. predicted	3. increased
4. predicted	5. picked	6. increased
7. was	8. was	9. thought
10. increased		

Summary of Actual Results From Table II (pg. 42)

1. compiled	2. compared	3. was
4. did	5. predicted	6. was
7. predicted	8. became	9. became
10. began	11. picked	12. increased
13. predicted		

Lexus's Explanation (pg. 43)

1. connected	2. wound	3. connected
4. flowed	5. wound	6. picked
7. wound	8. wound	9. picked
10. continued	11. wound	12. checked
13. picked	14. disconnected	15. wound
16. connected	17. checked	

Lexus's Summary (pg. 44–45)

1.	a.	was		
2.	b.	began	c.	wound
3.	d.	increased	e.	were
4.	f.	was		
5.	g.	used		
6.	h.	increased		
7.	i.	were	j.	was
8.	k.	were	l.	picked
9.	m.	added	n.	was
10.	o.	picked	p.	was
11.	q.	was	r.	was
12.	s.	was	t.	increased

13. 1, 4, 7, 8, 10, 11

Selecting the Best Written Summary of an Experiment (pg. 46–48)
Summaries A and B

1. B   2. B   3. B   4. B   5. A   6. B
Characteristics 1, 2, 3, 4, and 6 should be checked.

Summaries C and D

1. C   2. C   3. C   4. C   5. D   6. C   7. C
Characteristics 1, 2, 3, 4, 6, and 7 should be checked.

Chapter XII
Rocket Graph (pg. 49–50)
1. The rocket traveled 1,200 kilometers.
2. The rocket reached its high point of 60 kilometers half way through the flight.
3. The rocket was launched at 10:00 A.M.
4. The rocket landed at 11:00 A.M.
5. The rocket was in flight for one hour.
6. Answers will vary.

Earth/Sun Diagram (pg. 51–53)
T should be placed on 1, 3, 4, 7, 9, 10, 12, 14, 15, 17, 18, 20.
22. Answers will vary.

Interpreting Charts (pg. 54–56)
1. single	active	past
2.	active	present
3. single	active	present
4. single	active	past
5. single	active	present/past
6. single	active	present/past
7. single	active	past
8. single	active	present/past
9. single	active	present/past
10. single	active	past
11. single	passive	past

Sentence #	Voice	Tense	More Than One Point
2			p
3		t	
6		t	
7		t	
11	pv		

Chapter XIII
Joining Sentences Using Coordinating Conjunctions (pg. 57–58)
1. but, b
2. so, g
3. so, g
4. but, b
5. yet, f
6. so, g
7. and, a
8. but, b
9. for, c
10. so, g

Helping Danny Correct His Explanation (pg. 60–61)
1. a. is   b. want   c. is   d. can
   e. is   f. helps   g. comes   h. is
   i. find   j. is   k. shows   l. points
   m. points   n. receives   o. is
   p. determines   q. begins   r. receives
   s. is   t. is   u. receives
   v. means   w. is   x. is

2. A. but   B. and   C. and   D. so
   E. so   F. but   G. yet   H. so

Chapter XIV
Introduction (pg. 63–64)
a. 1. are
b. 2. are   3. do
c. 4. Do
d. 5. is   6. are   7. want   8. claim
   9. are
e. 10. was   11. was
f. 12. was

Method (pg. 65–67)
a. 1. 40 watts
   2. Company A
   3. $6.25
   4. $1.15
b. 1. toggle switch
   2. the same electrical outlet
   3. no
c. 1. 4:30 P.M. Wednesday
   2. 672
   3. $2.15
   4. $0.54
   5. past tense

Results (pg. 68)
1. at least 60%
2. Appendix A
3. approximately 75%
4. Appendix C

Discussion (pg. 69–70)
1. It was supported.
2. the compact fluorescent lightbulb
3. the incandescent lightbulb
4. They could run the experiment until the compact fluorescent lightbulb burned out.

Bibliography (pg. 70)
1. Pal Co-op
2. Matt Corand
3. August 12, 2008

Appendices (pg. 71)
1. three
2. Appendix A
3. Appendix C